SANTA CLAUS FOR ADULTS

SANTA CLAUS FOR ADULTS
Why God Doesn't Answer Your Prayers

RADYN RAMZY

COPYRIGHT © 2024 RADYN MEDIA
All rights reserved.

SANTA CLAUS FOR ADULTS
Why God Doesn't Answer Your Prayers

FIRST EDITION

ISBN   978-1-5445-4731-2 *Hardcover*
          978-1-5445-4730-5 *Paperback*
          978-1-5445-4729-9 *Ebook*

The Game

It's all just a Game,
with all the Game's Rules.

If you want to win,
you must play the Game,
with all the Game's Rules.

If you don't play by the Rules,
then you can't play the Game,
but how can you lose?

And in the end,
what do you really win
or lose?

After all,
it was only just a Game,
with all the Game's Rules.

—Radyn Ramzy, 1977

CONTENTS

PREFACE 9

1. FREEDOM TO BELIEVE 21
2. BROKEN PROMISES 45
3. THE INERRANT WORD OF GOD 63
4. TWO GODS, TWO BOOKS, TWO RELIGIONS 107
5. NEW TESTAMENT PROBLEMS 127
6. GOD'S LEADERSHIP 165
7. GENESIS REVISITED 195
8. WHAT IS THE TRUTH 237
9. GOLDEN NUGGETS 251

CONCLUSION 269

PREFACE

This is a book for people who are looking for the truth. Searching for the truth is a lot like mining for gold. It takes effort and some determination. You have to dig and sift through **a lot** of dirt to find those precious little nuggets. Most people aren't willing to put in that sort of effort. They'd rather watch TV and go to church once a week and let the preacher tell them everything they need to know. Unfortunately, that's not how you learn the truth. How do you know the preacher knows the truth? Just because he claims to? Just because he spends a half hour or so giving a good speech? Just because he can have you read a particular sentence in some chapter and verse that seems to back up what he is saying? That's not how you learn the truth. That's just believing in the preacher and *assuming* he knows what he's talking about.

Most people don't really start looking for the truth until they've experienced some pain. Like those who have felt the heart-rending anguish of losing something or someone that they believed was safe in God's hands. Those who have had their life ripped apart and now have to face day after lonely day without joy. Night after night, tossing and turning. No rest for your body, your mind, your heart, or your soul. Lying on a pillow soaked with tears. Or it may be dry, because there just aren't any tears left. If you don't know what I'm talking about, then maybe you're not ready to learn the truth. Then again, it might be a chance for you to avoid all that pain, by learning from other people's experiences about what you can expect from God.

It may have been your eyesight or your arm. It might have been your child or your spouse who will never reach the "golden years." Or it could've been your heart. Regardless of what it was, you never expected that God would have allowed it to happen. You believed His words when He said, *"Because you have made Yahweh your refuge, and the Most High your dwelling place, no evil shall happen to you, neither shall any plague come near your dwelling. For he will put his angels in charge of you, to guard you in all your ways"* (Psalm

91:9–11), and *"'For I know the plans I have for you,' declares the Lord, 'plans to prosper you and not to harm you, plans to give you hope and a future'"* (Jeremiah 29:11), and all the others—you know the words, you believed in them. And you prayed for His protection, His guidance. You tried to honor Him, follow Him, believe in Him, do His will… But yet, when the crises came, the promises turned up empty.

And now life will never be the same. The hopes and dreams you had will never be realized. The lifetime of love and happiness with the one you gave your heart to has ended, much sooner than you expected. The little one, your gift from heaven, is gone. She won't ever be a bride. He will never graduate. The goals you had been working towards, forever put out of reach by a body that can no longer function as it was designed to. Or by a disease that isn't going to allow you the time.

And then there are those few that made a choice. A conscious, determined choice to "have faith." You didn't have to. You knew you didn't. You could have gone the other way, and more than likely everything would have worked out quite well. You thought about it. You knew the options. But you decided to put your hope and trust in God and do it his way. You thought, *Surely, if I trust in Him and do as He asks, it will be OK. He won't let me down.* Right? After all, didn't He promise, *"And I will do whatever you ask in my name, so that the Father may be glorified in the Son. You may ask me for anything in my name, and I will do it"*? (John 14:13, 14) And now, not only are your dreams gone, the little that you had has been taken as well. How could it have ended up this way? You did what you were supposed to do. You did what He asked for. How can hell be the reward for doing the right thing?

The purpose of this book is to hopefully keep another person from making the mistake many other people have made. That mistake being making a life-changing decision based on the belief that there is a kind heavenly Father that loves you and will actually do what the Bible and its advocates claim He will do. Such as reward you for having faith, actually fulfill the promises made in the Bible, give you justice, answer your prayers, provide for your well-being and happiness, or heal a sick person. Despite all the promises, despite all the faith, despite all the prayers and tears, in case after case, there is no help from God. Lives are needlessly lost, and others ruined.

It's way past time to stand up and tell the truth. Those promises are just fantasies (and I'll tell you how to prove it for yourself). Putting faith in them and acting on that faith is a great way to ruin your life. If this book keeps just one person from making that mistake and spending the rest of their lives with the pain and regret that mistake brings, it will have served its purpose.

This book is not intended to be a definitive source of evidence or proof of the various topics discussed. I see no point, nor have any desire, to duplicate the excellent work done by so many others. Instead, honest seekers of the truth should consider this a rough guide and summary of the main points and concepts detailed in many other books and writings. Let the internet and/or whatever research tools you prefer help you find all the detailed information you need to draw your own conclusions as to the validity and correctness of the points I present.

Again, the main purpose of this book is to warn and hopefully keep anyone else from ever, Ever, EVER making a mistake that many others, including six million Jews, have found to be a fatal mistake; i.e., believing the words and promises in the Bible that tell of an all-powerful, all-knowing, all-loving God that will protect, provide, or bless you if you do what He says.

Since you don't know me from Adam, let me tell you a little about myself and where I'm coming from. For the purposes of this book, I chose the

Christian God rather than the God of some other religion simply because that's the one I believed in, the one I'm familiar with, and have read and pondered about the most. I've studied the Bible, extensively, and read many other books written by Christian and non-Christian writers on the subject of God, religion, the Bible, and their own experiences. I've also read other ancient writings and books about those ancient writings. I was raised in a conservative Christian household, attended private Christian schools, and was a believer for many years. So I also have my personal experience to draw from.

I'll give a quick summary of the progression of my self-education on religion. It started when, at age nineteen, I decided to read the Bible for myself to see what it actually said. I'd had years of church and church school teaching, but I had discovered that not everything I'd been taught was actually true. When I read the Bible for myself, I was literally surprised to find that it didn't actually say everything I'd been taught it said. And it also said a lot of things I'd never heard. I found that many of the verses that were used to "prove" the beliefs I'd been taught had been taken out of context, and then combined with other verses taken out of context, to create a belief that the Bible didn't actually support. Furthermore, I found verses that clearly contradicted some of those beliefs. I was shocked!

Over time, I read a lot of books written about the Bible and its teachings—most of them written by Christian authors such as C.S. Lewis (his *Mere Christianity* is a great book). I also read books written by "disillusioned" Christians, including some that were written by men that had been Christian pastors/preachers for many years. I read the books that were considered for inclusion in the Bible but wound up being left out, such as the books of the Apocrypha and the book of Enoch. I read other ancient writings, including the Egyptian *Book of the Dead* (I think all Christians should read that one) and various Sumerian texts.

One of the most impactful books I read was *The Age of Reason* by Thomas Paine, one of the founding fathers of America. It introduced me to the many examples of where the Bible contradicts itself. It was a bit of a tough read for me at the time because I was still a practicing Christian when I read it. Most of the book seems to be an all-out attack on the validity of the Bible, the Catholic Church, and the Christian God. But as I read it, I looked up the verses it was quoting, and verified for myself that they actually said what Thomas was claiming. And pretty much in each case, I had to admit he was correct. In the last two chapters, he finally explains that his motivation for pointing out flaws in the Bible is because the Bible is what the Catholic Church uses as the basis for their "God-given authority." And he absolutely despised the Catholic Church (for very good reasons). He actually did believe in the idea of a "higher power" (a Deity) and that we are held accountable (rewarded or punished) for our actions after we die.

From all my reading, I learned that the Bible had been both accidentally and purposedly mistranslated when compared to the original Hebrew and Greek texts. In many cases, it had been purposely mistranslated to support a belief that the original writings not only didn't support, but often clearly contradicted. That was another shocking discovery.

Then I began researching the history of the original texts. I learned that there are a large number of questions about when those texts were actually written and by whom. And which version of different copies of the original writings was the "right" one. Especially the New Testament. It's a total mess of different versions, unknown authors, and obvious additions and deletions of verses.

While I've found that modern Christian beliefs don't fit the facts, I do believe that at the beginning of human history, there were some beings that claimed to be, and were for all practical purposes, Gods. I believe that what we read in the Old Testament of the Bible and other ancient writings are stories about those "Gods" and their interactions with humans. While I believe the stories have been rather mangled and mythologized over time, I believe they are often based on facts and actual events. By considering them from that perspective, we can get a fairly decent view of the basic truth underlying them.

For the evolutionists and atheists who would like to use this book to bash religion and support their personal beliefs (which are every bit as much of a religion as any other), alas, I cannot help them. They are just as wrong and confused as any Christian or Muslim. Anyone that actually learns the facts of physics and biology knows it's impossible that the universe or life could have randomly and spontaneously "just happened." That Someone, or more likely many Someones, designed and created both is simply an unavoidable conclusion to any honest, knowledgeable person.

While many people might consider me to be an atheist, I don't. The definition of "atheist" is someone that denies the existence of God or of a supreme intelligent being. Unfortunately, most people that call themselves atheists have gone far beyond simply denying the existence of God to actively hating Christians, the Bible, and any suggestion of morals. As I stated above, it's simply not possible for life to have "naturally" begun on its own. Consequently, someone had to design and start it. But, just because those "Someones" may be far beyond us technologically doesn't mean they are "Gods" in any religious or spiritual sense.

There *is* one thing I admire about Charles Darwin, though. He had something that, apparently, none of his followers have; that is, the imagination to come up with an alternate explanation which, considering the level of knowledge at the time, seemed like a plausible theory. If his disciples had any honesty or imagination, they would admit that our current knowledge of biology and archeology proves the theory of evolution simply isn't true and come up with a new theory. Unfortunately, they are believers, not thinkers. Like most non-thinkers (true believers), all they can see are two possibilities. It's either evolution or biblical creation. They're too dim to realize there might be a third option and too unimaginative to come up with one.

Most believers, regardless of what their belief is, are simply too ignorant to know they are wrong. I use the term "ignorant" to mean a lack of knowledge (which is exactly what it means). Unfortunately, not only are they ignorant, they are also willfully ignorant. They don't really want to know they are wrong. They also don't want to spend the time and effort to gain knowledge to prove whether they are right or wrong. They'd much rather just kick back and listen to their teacher, preacher, parent, or friend and accept whatever they say as the truth. Some "believers" (usually the leaders and biggest proponents of the "faith") actually know it's not true, but they teach it and preach it anyway because it serves their interest, which is often a personal financial interest.

Hopefully you're beginning to realize I'm not writing this because I'm some evil atheist that hates the concept of God or Christianity. I'm not. I think in our modern world, Christians are generally pretty good people, good citizens, and good neighbors. But I hate being deceived and seeing people get hurt because they don't know the truth.

While this is not a long book, it does represent what I've spent countless hours researching, studying, thinking about, and learning over a lifetime. As with all knowledge, there's two ways to learn it: the slow hard way, which is learning by experience, or the quick easy way, which is by reading the knowledge others have accumulated the slow hard way. Which method you choose is up to you. But I will point out that you will not live long enough to learn the hard way, even a fraction of the knowledge humans have accumulated up to this point. Furthermore, by learning the quick, easy way, you have a much greater chance of living a successful life, especially when you consider that you will be competing with others that *will* take the quick and easy way.

In this short book, which anyone should be able to read in a day or two, you can save years of time and effort learning what took me a lifetime to learn. I must admit, my current beliefs, based on what I've learned, certainly aren't the conclusion I would have expected when I started my search.

CHAPTER 1

FREEDOM TO BELIEVE

Belief is a very powerful thing. Unfortunately, it doesn't matter whether the belief is true or not. There is a great amount of power, even in a false belief. I will point out some examples where a false belief can result in good benefits. Having a positive attitude because you believe an almighty Allah is helping and supporting you will increase your chances of success. It's the positive attitude, however, that actually causes the effect, not Allah. But if a person can't have a positive attitude without their belief in Allah, then their belief in a nonexistent God does provide some benefit. Alcoholics Anonymous is a great example of this. The organization encourages its members to believe in a "higher power of their own choosing," and then they request the help and support of that "higher power" in their battle against addiction. And it works! I heard that one member chose doorknobs as his higher power because there were doorknobs almost everywhere he went. So, in his mind, he could find and see his higher power almost anywhere. While I'm pretty sure most people would agree that doorknobs are not Gods, for that particular alcoholic, that belief worked.

For the most part, people are free to believe whatever they wish and, for the most part, I support people's right to freedom of belief. But believing things that aren't true will usually lead to outcomes that are not beneficial for the believer. Nor for the rest of society when those believers have the power to impose their will on others. History is littered with many millions of murdered people simply because they didn't happen to believe what those in power wanted them to believe. Nazi Germany and Communist Russia are a couple of the most significant recent examples.

What we believe is probably the largest determining factor that shapes our lives. Our beliefs determine how and, to a large extent, what we think and feel. In turn, our thoughts and feelings determine our actions. Finally, our actions, for the most part, determine our success or lack thereof. This is an example of the law of cause and effect.

So, how do we know what to believe? How do we determine what the truth actually is? When we look at history and our modern societies, we find a fairly consistent example of one method of determining the truth: the court system. While we can find plenty of examples of cases where courts have failed, so far no one seems to have come up with a better method.

So, just for the sake of a thought experiment, imagine that you are a judge. The case before you at the moment is a murder case where a conviction will result in the execution of the accused person. You don't know the murder victim or the person being accused of the murder, nor do you know any information about the murder itself. How then are you going to be able to make a determination of guilt or innocence? Hopefully, you would, honestly and objectively, listen to the evidence and arguments presented by *both* those pushing for a conviction and those pushing for an acquittal. And after carefully considering all of the evidence and arguments provided by *both* sides, you would conclude whether the evidence of guilt reached the level of "beyond a reasonable doubt." You have someone's life in your hands. It would be terrible to execute an innocent person, but it would also be terrible to let a murderer escape justice.

Ideally, we would follow the same process when it comes to what we believe. Spend a little effort researching and considering the evidence *both* for and against something presented as a "truth." Unfortunately, that's not what usually happens. What normally happens is we are told something from some sort of "authority" and just accept it as true. That's understandable since that is the way we are taught from birth to adulthood. Our parents, teachers, and other adults (even older kids), whether consciously or not, are considered "authorities," and we naturally tend to believe what they tell us. After plus or minus twenty years of this type of learning, it's not surprising that most people tend to continue "learning" that way for the rest of their lives. Unfortunately, it's also how all sorts of lies, nonsense, and superstition wind up being believed by vast numbers of people.

Imagine a judge that would only allow or consider evidence from the defense attorney, refusing to allow or consider anything the prosecution tried to present. Would you consider that a fair trial? Do you think a judgment in that case would represent the truth? If you were the judge, would you do that? Hopefully, any honest, fair-minded person will recognize that coming to a conclusion when you've only examined one side of the evidence can't possibly be a valid method for discovering the truth. Furthermore, any "truth" (belief) that can't stand up to cross-examination or questioning can't possibly be the truth. Or at least certainly not the whole truth. Real truth isn't threatened by questions or debate, or even the majority belief. The only threat to real truth is ignorance and those that use the ignorance of the majority to attack and destroy those that know the truth.

If you stop and think about it, how many times have you met someone that held a false belief simply because they'd never heard or honestly considered the evidence against that belief? For that matter, how many beliefs do you hold that have never been honestly examined? Beliefs where you've never considered, or even allowed, any contrary evidence to be presented?

Many religions severely warn against reading or listening to anything other than the officially approved documents or their religious representatives. In fact, many warn against even coming to your own conclusion based on your personal understanding of the officially approved documents. Most of these warnings are framed like "you must not allow the devil to gain any access to your mind by any means whatsoever," such as reading, watching, or listening to (much less considering) any information from any source other than the official sources. "Solo scriptura" (by the Bible alone) is a good example of this.

If any person or organization can convince you to believe only what they say and to refuse to consider any opposing voices or evidence, they can get you to believe anything they want. This is how we get cult leaders like Jim Jones and David Koresh. Murderous nations like Hitler and the Nazis; Karl Marx, Joseph Stalin, and the Communists. Murderous medieval kings of many nations around the world. Virtually all religions. Moses and the Hebrews. Jesus and the Christians. Mohamed and the Muslims. The Pope and Catholics. Martin Luther and Lutherans. Joseph Smith and Mormons. Ellen G. White and Seventh-day Adventists. And on and on.

The key is to keep the believers from considering any evidence or even ideas from the "outside." And as history has repeatedly shown, if the organization has the power, then they use all means of persuasion, even to the extent of torture and murder, to eliminate any dissent. If you stop and consider the number of deaths that many of those organizations I mentioned above are responsible for, then it should become blatantly clear that limiting the information you will consider as true to a single source is not the path to wisdom, or the truth. Don't be afraid of reading or hearing lies. Instead, learn how to test them with evidence and reason. Eventually, you will get quite good at quickly recognizing lies and misinformation.

Humans have a wondrous ability to believe almost anything. I'm sure you've been surprised by some of the things people have told you that they actually believed are true. Even a cursory review of history will reveal many strange things that people have believed. And not just a few people, but the vast majority of the people at the time believed them, including the so-called experts and scientists...even preachers.

Two ideas were that the world was flat or that Incans, Indonesians, and others needed to make human sacrifices to the Volcano God so that he wouldn't get angry and destroy them all. Or that heavier-than-air flight was impossible—a supposed "scientific fact" prior to the invention of the airplane. I find that one especially confusing. Those "scientists" were surrounded by birds. I know they saw them. And even though they might not have had the tools we have today, what they did have was way more than sufficient to weigh an eagle and know, beyond a shadow of a doubt, that it was heavier than air. And they could see it fly. There's no way to deny that. So, how in the world could it have possibly been a "scientific fact" that heavier-than-air flight was impossible? That's ridiculous. When you consider various beliefs throughout history, or even all of the different things people believe today, it becomes quite obvious that people can, and do, believe almost anything they want.

Another reason people believe all sorts of garbage is because most don't know how to think logically.

Logical reasoning is not something that humans do naturally. It is a learned skill and, unfortunately, it's not taught in school. I heard Steve Jobs (one of the founders and CEO of Apple corporation) in an interview make a very profound statement. He said that kids should be taught computer programming in school. *Not for the purpose of teaching them how to program, but simply so they can learn how to think*. Computer programming requires learning how to think logically. Logical thinking is what is meant by the terms "reasoning" and "critical thinking." It's the only reliable method of consistently arriving at a correct conclusion. But as I said, it's not something most people ever learn how to do—which goes a long way in explaining how so many people can believe so many things that are simply not true.

I discovered an interesting fact many years ago. I found that it's impossible to believe something that you *know* is not true. Go ahead and try it. Try to make yourself believe that the moon doesn't exist. You can *argue* that the moon doesn't exist, you can *tell other people* you don't believe it exists, you can even *teach* people that the moon doesn't exist. But you'll find that you can't actually believe it yourself. Because you can see it and you *know* that it does exist.

People can only believe something as long as they don't actually *know* it's not true. A major university did a study several years ago, looking into the process of changing someone's beliefs. The study consisted of two phases. In step one of the first phase, a group of volunteer students who had never studied astronomy were given a questionnaire asking how our solar system works. While most of their answers were wrong, they all had some concept of how our solar system works. For step two, the volunteers were enrolled in a quarter-long course in which they learned how our solar system actually worked. At the end of the class, they took a final exam. Everyone passed. Then, for step three, the students were given the exact same final exam six months later. Surprisingly, the vast majority of them had reverted to their original mistaken concepts of how the solar system works. Somehow, they had managed to forget what they had learned in that class.

In phase two of the study, the researchers took a new group of volunteers who had never studied astronomy and gave them the same questionnaire. Just as in phase one, while they all had some concept of how the solar system works, most of them were wrong. For step two, they again had the volunteers take the same course on how the solar system works. But this time, they spent the first couple of weeks reviewing the volunteers' mistaken ideas from the questionnaire and explaining *how and why* those ideas were *wrong*. At the end of the course, they again gave the volunteers a final exam, and again everyone passed. Just as in phase one, after six months, they gave the volunteers the exact same final exam. This time almost all of them passed. Hardly anyone had returned to their original beliefs.

From repeated experiments, they found that *unless you first convince someone that their current beliefs are wrong, it usually doesn't do any good to teach them the truth*. Even if they believe the new information, after a fairly short period, most people will return to their original wrong belief. This confirmed the fact I had discovered: you can't believe something you know isn't true. Once convinced that their original beliefs were wrong, there was no way for the volunteers to return to a belief that they *knew* wasn't true.

Like children finding out Santa Claus isn't real, we've all had the surprising experience of learning that something we believed wasn't actually the truth. It might have been something small, like learning that oil doesn't actually come from dead dinosaurs (as of 2022 the US alone used nearly twenty million barrels of oil *per day*![1] The worldwide use was ninety-seven million barrels

---

1   "How Much Oil Is Consumed in the United States," U.S. Energy Information Administration, updated September 22, 2023, https://www.eia.gov/tools/faqs/faq.php?id=33&t=6.

per day![2] No matter how many dinosaurs you may think there were, it's not even remotely possible that there were *ever* enough dinosaurs to provide even a single year's worth of oil at that rate of consumption.). Or it might be something a bit more alarming, like finding out your spouse hasn't been as faithful as you believed. If you ponder these experiences and stop and consider *why* your belief was wrong, you will generally find it's one of two basic reasons: either someone gave you wrong information that you didn't verify, or you just assumed something was true. Both of those are caused by ignorance (lack of knowledge).

Even more surprising, when we first experience it, is the realization that people will actually purposely lie to us, including people that supposedly love you. Here in America, being deceived by loved ones starts almost as soon as we begin to comprehend words. Our parents start teaching us little fantasies (lies) like the Easter Bunny, the Tooth Fairy, and Santa Claus. While those are admittedly pretty harmless deceptions (everyone knows the child is going to learn the truth sooner or later), it's still an odd practice when you ponder the fact that we are lying to a completely innocent, trusting child. For those who seek the truth, it seems like life is

---

[2] "Oil Consumption Worldwide from 1998 to 2023," Statista, July 15, 2024, https://www.statista.com/statistics/265239/global-oil-consumption-in-barrels-per-day.

a long series of learning that what we were told or taught was horsepucky. We slowly learn that we can't trust our parents, teachers, doctors, priests, or government. In many cases, it's not that they meant to lie to us, they simply believed the wrong information that had been taught to them. If you haven't discovered this yet, then maybe this book can begin to open your eyes.

One of the more elaborate and effective stories that has been taught for thousands of years is that there is an all-knowing, all-powerful God that created the entire universe and every living thing in it, including us. The specific characteristics of this God have evolved over the centuries into the kind, loving, heavenly Father that is taught in modern Christianity today. This is the ultimate Santa Claus story—Santa Claus for adults.

According to the Pew Research Center, as of 2018, 90 percent of Americans believe in either the God of the Bible or some other higher power. Fifty-six percent believe in the God of the Bible.[3] Let's take a look at why people believe this story and how they maintain that belief in spite of clear evidence to the contrary.

---

[3] Dalia Fahmy, "Key Findings about Americans' Belief in God," Pew Research Center, April 25, 2018, https://www.pewresearch.org/short-reads/2018/04/25/key-findings-about-americans-belief-in-god/.

It's important to realize that this story is thousands of years old. It's been passed on from one generation to the next. Its evangelists have spread it all over the earth. Its proponents and teachers have put centuries' worth of effort into perfecting their sales pitch and dealing with all those inconvenient verses and real-life experiences that might cast doubt on its validity. They have written thousands of books arguing their case and explaining away the opposing evidence. It's big business and the sole source of income for a lot of people. For some of those people, it's a *really nice* income. (I have no problem with people earning a living or even making a lot of money from religion, but we should at least acknowledge the motivation that it creates.)

With that background, it shouldn't be surprising that most American and European Christians inherited their beliefs. It's what their parents believed. It's what the majority of the society they live in believes. It's what they've been taught from birth. Even those who don't practice the religion at least understand the basic ideas and tend to believe some of it.

If it's not true, how do that many people maintain their belief? How does that work? Let's look at prayer and the psychology of positive reinforcement. Prayer is a powerful reinforcement for the believer, as long as they're careful what they pray for.

Most believers ask God to keep all of their loved ones safe, probably every day. So, statistically, for someone that only loses a single loved one over the course of a year, God answered their prayer 364 out of 365 days! That's pretty good success! And if the loved one they lost wasn't an immediate family member or dear friend or was someone that was old or had a long-term illness, although it is a sad loss, it's not an absolute heart crusher. It's not the same level of grief we experience from the unexpected loss of a spouse or child—the kind of grief that may wound our soul and cause us to wonder why God would allow this.

When looking for work, most believers will ask God to help them get a job. Then they send out resumes, talk to businesses they'd like to work for, and use social networking to contact others that help support their efforts. Sure enough, sooner or later, they get a job! And when they do, they thank God for providing it to them. More reinforcement.

After a couple minutes of looking, many believers will ask God to help them find their keys, glasses, or the TV remote. Then they continue looking and 99 percent of the time they *do* find whatever it was they were looking for! A 99-percent success rate definitely helps the believability factor.

As every believer knows, you don't get everything you ask for. They've all been taught that "God isn't a vending machine," "Some of God's greatest gifts are unanswered prayers," and sometimes "God, in his infinite wisdom, just says no." The point is they aren't really expecting 100 percent success, which leads to an interesting study I read about a number of years ago.

One of the major universities, I think it was Harvard, did a study on positive reinforcement using rats. I realize humans aren't rats, but a lot of psychological behaviors are quite common across a wide range of animals, including humans.

To conduct the study, the researchers conducted an experiment using a simple T-shaped rat run with a button at the left and right end of the T. In the first step of the experiment, the buttons didn't do anything. They would put a rat into the end of the T and then see whether it would go left or right when it got to the T intersection. This was done quite a few times with many rats. As expected, it was close to a 50/50 chance whether the rats would go left or right.

In the next step of the experiment, the experimenters activated the button at the right end of the T, which would deliver a single treat when the rat pushed it. The rats quickly learned they could get a treat by going right and pushing the button. Once they learned that, they would turn right at the T intersection 100 percent of the time.

The final step of the experiment was to deactivate the treat button and see how long it took for the rats to go back to a 50/50 chance of turning right or left at the T intersection. I don't remember exactly how long it was (and it's not really important), but it was quite a while. The most interesting results came from the next phase of the study.

For this phase, a new batch of rats was used in the same experiment except for one minor difference. In the step of the experiment where the right-hand button was activated to deliver a treat, it would only deliver a treat once out of every four times it was pressed. Again, the rats quickly learned they could get a treat by turning right and pressing the button. Even though it would only deliver a treat once out of every four times, they would turn right at the T intersection 100 percent of the time.

It's in the final step where things really get interesting. This time, when they deactivated the treat button it took *four times as long* for the rats to go back to a 50/50 chance of turning right or left at the T intersection! In other words, occasional success creates a much longer-lasting behavior (or belief) modification than 100 percent success.

With that in mind, let's go back to prayer. Based on the rat study, the fact that believers don't get everything they ask for just helps reinforce the practice of praying. In addition, as I pointed out in my examples of prayer earlier, you can have a really good rate of success with prayer if you're careful what you pray for. Imagine the prayer success you would have if you asked God every night to make the sun come up the next morning. You would have had 100 percent success with that prayer for your entire life so far!

This is a very important point. Let's review the prayer examples I gave earlier.

Praying for loved ones to be kept safe. As we all know, 100 percent of us die sooner or later. Consequently, sooner or later the prayer to keep a particular loved one safe is not going to be answered affirmatively. Any adult understands this, so the prayer to keep loved ones safe is really just a prayer to let them have at least a normal life span with no major physical catastrophes such as some terminal disease, an accident that leaves them permanently maimed, or even things like an economic disaster. Is there any evidence that people who someone prays for to keep them safe are actually kept any "safer" than people that don't have anyone praying to keep them safe? While I haven't seen any studies or statistics on this, I tend to doubt that statistically there's any difference. But as I pointed out earlier, until something unpleasant and unexpected happens to one of those loved ones, people can believe that God is answering their prayers whether He is or not.

Praying for help finding a job. While people may believe God helped them land a new job, is there any evidence that that is actually the case? What about all the people that get a new job without asking for God's help? Is there any difference in the success rate between the two groups?

Praying for help finding keys, glasses, or the TV remote. For people that make this kind of prayer, think about where you actually found whatever it was you were looking for after you asked for God's help. What are the chances you would have found it anyway had you just kept looking? I myself used to make these types of prayers. Since I quit, I haven't spent any more time or had any more trouble finding things than I did before. In fact, if anything, I've had less trouble because I've gotten better at making sure I put things "where they belong" when I'm done with them.

The truth is, without any studies and objective statistics for all of those prayers, there's not really any way to tell whether God is actually doing anything for you. Of course, the beauty for believers is, without any objective measurement, there's no way to prove He isn't either. This is how the fantasy is maintained. Since there's no way to *know* for a fact that God isn't helping you, you're free to believe that He is. *As long as you're careful what you ask for.*

The only time believers will run into problems with prayer is when they try praying for something that can *only* happen if God actually intervenes. They all probably try it. And when they don't get the results they asked for, they console themselves with all the seemingly reasonable explanations for failure that the religious leaders have been making up for centuries. Generally, they assume the failure is somehow their fault. Either they aren't righteous enough for God to grant their desire, or they just don't have enough faith, or maybe they shouldn't have had that desire in the first place and God is trying to help them get rid of it. Or it could be that they just don't have the ability to see the long-term consequences of whatever it is they wanted, and by not giving it to them God is actually just protecting them from themselves. There's a never-ending list of rationales and excuses.

Unfortunately, for the believers that actually study the Bible, they will find verses like Mark 11:24 where Jesus says, *"Therefore I tell you, whatever you ask for in prayer, believe that you have received it, and it will be yours."* Or Matthew 18:19, where he says, *"Again I say to you, if two of you agree on earth about anything they ask, it will be done for them by my Father in heaven."* There's not a lot of ambiguity in that verse. It quite clearly states that *it will be done*!

And here is how you can prove how much faith you should put in what the Bible says. Take another believer you feel comfortable with and go to the local hospital. Find a child with a terminal illness like cancer, and then the two of you agree that the child should have a chance to live a normal lifespan. Then ask God to heal the child in accordance with the verse above in Matthew. If it doesn't work, do it with some other believer. Or with lots of other believers. Do it for other patients.

If none of that works, get the "elders" (deacons, pastors, priests, bishops, or whatever the church leaders are called in your denomination) and have them go anoint the person(s) in accordance with James 5:14–15: *"Is anyone among you sick? Let them call the elders of the church to pray over them and anoint them with oil in the name of the Lord. And the prayer offered in faith will make the sick person well; the Lord will raise him up. If he has sinned, he will be forgiven."*

I know most believers aren't actually going to do any of this, and the "elders" aren't going to be too wild about it either. Odds are pretty good that the "elders" will "explain" why those verses don't actually mean what they say, or why they no longer apply. Remember, they have centuries of experience dodging these types of issues. One of their favorites is to insist that whenever you ask for something, you always ask "according to God's will." That way, if it doesn't work, it obviously wasn't God's will. But if you notice, those verses don't instruct you to ask according to God's will. They simply state that if you do what it says, God will make it happen.

If the "elders" actually do the anointing, they might do it once or twice, but when it doesn't work, they're *definitely* going to find a "good reason" to quit. It quickly gets embarrassing when you do what the Bible says but don't get the result it says you will. For the "elders," that might cause the flock to start asking uncomfortable questions. That wouldn't be good.

If someone you prayed for actually does get better, keep in mind that it's a well-known fact that occasionally a patient with a terminal illness, like cancer, will experience spontaneous remission. It happens fairly often. Up to 22 percent of breast cancer cases went into spontaneous remission, according to one carefully done study.[4]

So, to be certain that it's actually God answering the prayers, the success rate would need to be higher than the known rate of spontaneous remission. I would point out that the verses above don't say "occasionally it will be done" or "sometimes the sick person will get well." Taking those verses at face value, it would be reasonable to expect a 100 percent success rate.

Although it would be less than what the verses indicate, if prayer healed even half of the people prayed for, I would consider that a huge success and undeniable evidence that someone, or something, was indeed answering those prayers. In fact, I'm sure the vast majority of people would consider it pretty good evidence that God was healing people. Sadly, I'm also quite confident that doesn't and isn't going to happen. I really wish it did and would. I wish there really was a kind, loving, heavenly Father that actually did what the Bible says

---

[4] Per-Henrik Zahl, Jan Mæhlen, and H. Gilbert Welch, "The Natural History of Invasive Breast Cancers Detected by Screening Mammography," *Archives of Internal Medicine* 168, no. 21 (November 24, 2008): 2311–2316, https://doi.org/10.1001/archinte.168.21.2311.

He will do. A God that had a plan for your life. That would bless and prosper the good people and punish the evil ones. Unfortunately, that's not what we see when we consider the world today…or the world of the past. In the next chapter, we will look at people that put all of their faith in God and what the Bible claims He would do.

CHAPTER 2

BROKEN PROMISES

Years ago, there was a Christian organization for men called Promise Keepers. The purpose of the organization was to teach and encourage men to become men of honor and integrity. Men you could count on. Men whose word you could trust and rely on. Men that would make a promise and keep it. Men that emulated God. It was a noble goal, and wouldn't it be nice if everyone was like that?

Nobody likes a promise breaker. Politicians, lawyers, used car salesmen—these are groups that, right or wrong, most people don't have a lot of respect for because they are considered to have an above-average percentage of liars in them. People you can't really trust. People that will say one thing and do another. People that will make promises they don't keep—and never intended to keep.

Broken promises hurt. Whether it's a huge promise like "I do" or a smaller promise like "I'll be at your soccer game," each one diminishes our faith not only in that person but, over time, in all of humanity as well. But we can always trust in God, right?

A broken promise is just a lie. Actually, it's one of the worst types of lies. It's a lie that someone guarantees with their integrity. What kind of person makes promises they don't keep? It's a very unpleasant experience when a promise you've believed in and acted on turns out to be a lie. As every divorcee knows, one of the worst is when someone breaks the promise they made with the words "I do."

Anytime you care to look, you can read cases where someone, usually a child, has died because normal medical treatment was refused in favor of prayer and faith in God. Search the internet and read some of the stories. It is well worth the time. Stories about babies dying from a simple infection while the parents prayed. Diabetic children dying because their parents refused to give them insulin because the Bible says God would heal them if they just had faith and that using insulin would demonstrate a lack of faith. Other children dying or being permanently damaged by things easily fixed with common surgical procedures. From infants to adults, a lot of people have died because they or their "guardians" believed the promises they read in the Bible. *Truly believed with all their heart and mind* that God would actually honor those promises.

The following excerpt is from an article in *The Guardian*, April 13, 2016:

> Mariah Walton's voice is quiet—her lungs have been wrecked by her illness, and her respirator doesn't help. But her tone is resolute.
>
> "Yes, I would like to see my parents prosecuted."
>
> Why?
>
> "They deserve it." She pauses. "And it might stop others."
>
> Mariah is 20 but she's frail and permanently disabled. She has pulmonary hypertension and when she's not bedridden, she has to carry an oxygen tank that allows her to breathe. At times, she has had screws in her bones to anchor her breathing device. She may soon have no option for a cure except a heart and lung transplant–an extremely risky procedure.

All this could have been prevented in her infancy by closing a small congenital hole in her heart. It could even have been successfully treated in later years, before irreversible damage was done. But Mariah's parents were fundamentalist Mormons who went off the grid in northern Idaho in the 1990s and refused to take their children to doctors, believing that illnesses could be healed through faith and the power of prayer.

As she grew sicker and sicker, Mariah's parents would pray over her and use alternative medicine.[5]

From an article in *Time*, February 5, 2009:

On Easter Sunday of 2008, 11-year-old Kara Neumann of Weston, Wisconsin, suffered waves of nausea as she lay motionless on her deathbed, too weak to walk or speak. Kara's parents, both followers of the Unleavened Bread Ministries, an online church that shuns medical intervention, knelt in prayer beside their dying daughter. They did not call a doctor for help. A few hours later Kara died of diabetes. A common, and treatable, condition.[6]

---

5   Jason Wilson, "Letting Them Die: Parents Refuse Medical Help for Children in the Name of Christ," *The Guardian*, April 13, 2016, https://www.theguardian.com/us-news/2016/apr/13/followers-of-christ-idaho-religious-sect-child-mortality-refusing-medical-help.

6   Deena Gudzer, "When Parents Call God Instead of the Doctor," *Time*, February 5, 2009, https://time.com/archive/6914048/when-parents-call-god-instead-of-the-doctor/.

From an article in *The Objective Standard*, July 7, 2013:

> Seven-month-old Brandon Schaible died from bacterial pneumonia, severe dehydration, and strep while his parents watched and prayed and, in accordance with their religious beliefs, refused to provide the child with medicine.
>
> The atrocity is magnified by the fact that Brandon was the second Schaible child to die this way from bacterial pneumonia and religiously motivated lack of medical treatment.[7]

From an article in *The Telegraph*, November 6, 2007:

> A Jehovah's Witness died shortly after giving birth to twins because her faith prevented her from having a blood transfusion. Emma Gough, 22, began hemorrhaging but because her beliefs did not allow her to receive blood she slipped into unconsciousness and died.
>
> As she suffered severe blood loss and her life ebbed away, medical staff urged her husband Anthony, and

---

[7] Natalie Ogle, "Death by Prayer: Christian Fundamentalist Parents Denied Their Children Medicine and Watched Them Die," *The Objective Standard*, July 7, 2013, https://theobjectivestandard.com/2013/07/death-by-prayer-christian-fundamentalist-parents-denied-their-children-medicine-and-watched-them-die/.

her parents, all of whom follow the same faith, to overrule her decision and allow a transfusion which could have saved her. But they refused.[8]

From Religious Tolerance:

Some cases of apparently preventable deaths due to reliance on faith healing by Christian Scientist parents are:

Ashley King died in 1988 at the age of twelve. Her parents, John and Catherine King, had withdrawn her from her Phoenix, Arizona, school in 1987 because of "a problem with her leg." CPS gained temporary custody of the child and took her to the hospital. She had a tumor on her right leg that was forty-one inches in circumference. The attending doctor estimated that she would have had a fifty-five to 60 percent chance of recovery if she had received prompt medical attention earlier. He recommended that her leg be amputated "to reduce her pain in the time she had remaining." The parents refused and transferred her to a Christian Science nursing home where she received only non-medical care. Most such nursing homes do not permit distribution of pain medication. She allegedly died in extreme pain.

---

8   Nick Britten, "Mother Dies After Refusing Blood Transfusion," *The Telegraph*, November 6, 2007, https://www.telegraph.co.uk/news/uknews/1568447/Mother-dies-after-refusing-blood-transfusion.html.

Robyn Twitchell of Boston, Massachusetts, died in 1986 at the age of two of an intestinal blockage which could have been repaired by conventional surgery.

Amy Hermanson, age seven, died from childhood diabetes. Her Sarasota, Florida, parents are Christian Scientists. They were aware of her illness but did not seek medical attention for her.

Andrew Wantland, age twelve, died of untreated juvenile diabetes in Orange County, California. He had lost weight, complained of exhaustion, and drank large amounts of water—all indications of diabetes. After missing a week of schooling due to what his family called the "flu," Andrew's father finally summoned an ambulance. He was pronounced dead on arrival at the hospital.[9]

Rita Swan co-founded Children's Healthcare Is a Legal Duty (CHILD) in 1983. According to CHILD, about **three hundred children die each year because of their parents' religious beliefs**.[10]

---

9 Quoted by user Formaldehyde, "Judge Rules Family Can't Refuse Chemo for Boy," forum, May 19, 2009, https://forums.civfanatics.com/threads/judge-rules-family-cant-refuse-chemo-for-boy.321464/.

10 Massachusetts Citizens for Children, "Death by Religious Exemption," *MassKids*, accessed July 6, 2024, https://www.masskids.org/index.php/religiously-motivated-medical-neglect/death-by-religious-exemption.

Faith Assembly is a church active in Ohio and Indiana. According to research by CHILD, there have been over one hundred unnecessary deaths since 1973 caused by the teachings of the church against medical care. The majority of these deaths have been of children or mothers in childbirth.[11]

Faith Assembly death rates were studied from 1975–1982 by the US Centers for Disease Control and the Indiana Department of Health. Death rates among Faith Assembly women in childbirth were 870 percent higher than among Indiana women in general. Death rates among their infants were 270 percent higher than the statewide average.[12]

Swan documented deaths of children in Christian Science families due to:

> ...meningitis, diabetes, diphtheria, measles, kidney infection, septicemia, cancer, and appendicitis. She has found outbreaks of polio and measles at Christian Science camps and schools. She has interviewed adults who, because of diseases and injuries that went untreated during childhood,

---

[11] Massachusetts Citizens for Children, "Death by Religious Exemption."
[12] Massachusetts Citizens for Children, "Death by Religious Exemption."

became deaf, or lame, or suffered permanent organ damage.[13]

Most believers react with sadness, irritation, and confusion as to why someone would do these things. I ask, with all sincerity, if they truly believe in the Bible, why doesn't every believer do it? If they actually believed the Bible was the word of God, why *wouldn't* they let God keep His promises, reveal His glory, and heal the sick person? Which is the true believer? The one that runs to the doctor or the one that puts their faith in God?

For those who would imply that anyone who would do such a thing must be ignorant, deceived, or perhaps just evil, I would remind you of the great Biblical patriarch Abraham. He was going to *kill* his child because he believed God told him to. To Abraham, God and His command were more important than the life of his child. None of these parents let their children die because they didn't love their children. They did it because, like Abraham, they believed they were putting God first and obeying His will. They put *all* of their faith in God's promises—and lost. Sad but true…

---

13 Rajesh Tehankar et al., "Implications and Challenges of Genetic Counselling of Tribal Families with Down's Syndrome in Central India," *Journal of Evolution of Medical and Dental Sciences* 3, no. 37 (2014): 9627–9632, http://dx.doi.org/10.14260/jemds/2014/3246.

And who, exactly, is responsible for the deaths by prayer? "The parents" would be the obvious answer. But what about the preachers, teachers, and authors that promote and support the beliefs those parents acted on? And while those people are certainly complicit, even they are simply "spreading the good news" of the wonderful promises written in the Bible, the very Word of God.

The promises were actually written by various men, and many of them are supposedly direct quotes from Jesus, who, according to John 1:1, was the very Word of God itself made into human form. Not only was he the Word of God, according to John, he *was* God. So, the promises that those parents bet the life of their child on, according to the Bible, came from God himself. Again, I ask, who exactly is responsible for the deaths by prayer?

Most believers know better. They know that the only time you put all of your hope in God is when there simply is no other option. The experience of unanswered prayers and unfulfilled promises becomes so common that they don't even really think about it anymore. Failure is just accepted as normal. But if you ask them, they will tell you they believe God *does* answer prayer and fulfill his promises. They never seem to notice the dichotomy between their beliefs and the results.

Of course, it doesn't help when all of the teachers, preachers, and authors explain how unfulfilled promises are some of God's greatest gifts. Just God in his infinite wisdom protecting you from your own stupidity. Or a million and one other excuses as to why the promise failed. One of the most insidious excuses is that the failure is due to a lack of faith on the part of the believer. How much faith does it take to bet on your life or the life of someone you love?

Another common explanation given for why the promises fail when people don't use standard medical practices is that God has given us our modern medical knowledge and we should use it rather than ask God for a miracle. But let's consider diabetes. Insulin is like a crutch. It's not a cure. It doesn't solve the problem. At best, it just helps you live with it. Sooner or later the diabetes is going to cause other issues which will eventually kill you. Although the American Medical Association doesn't admit it, diabetes is the third leading cause of death in America.[14] Why should a Christian settle for a lifetime of trying to manage a

---

14 According to the CDC (in the US) and the WHO (worldwide), it's the eighth leading cause of death. See National Center for Health Statistics, "Leading Causes of Death," Centers for Disease Control, reviewed May 2, 024, https://www.cdc.gov/nchs/fastats/leading-causes-of-death.htm; World Health Organization, "The Top 10 Causes of Death," August 7, 2024, https://www.who.int/news-room/fact-sheets/detail/the-top-10-causes-of-death.

disease when God himself has promised them that prayer and faith will heal them? And what about all of the other diseases which modern medicine has no answer for? What is the believer supposed to do when facing one of those?

Anyone who has been a believer and attended church for a while has had the experience of some church member being diagnosed with a terminal disease, such as cancer. Usually, it will be announced during church services, and people will be asked to pray for the sick person. And they do pray. And they "claim" the promises written in the Bible.

In some churches, elders will "anoint" the sick person as directed in James 5:14–15: *"Is anyone among you sick? Let him call for the elders of the church, and let them pray over him, anointing him with oil in the name of the Lord. And the prayer of faith will save the one who is sick, and the Lord will raise him up. And if he has committed sins, he will be forgiven."*

Unfortunately, as anyone that's tried it has learned, it doesn't work. After participating in or even just observing the process a few times, we learn that it's just another religious ritual we go through. Of course, everyone always *hopes* it will work, we wish really hard, but in the end, no one, except the new believers, is terribly surprised when it doesn't. We *hear* stories of it working; it just never seems to happen here.

Besides cases of children dying because of misguided parental beliefs, with a little more research you can find plenty of cases where people have learned the hard way that God's promises are not something you want to bet your future on.

One of the greatest examples of this is the six million Jews slaughtered during World War II because they didn't leave when they could have and then didn't fight back when it was too late to escape. In multiple interviews with Jewish survivors of the Holocaust, I've heard them explain how they believed that, surely, God would protect them just as the Bible said He would. I've also heard many of them say they will never make that mistake again.

How many people have died or had their lives ruined because they made choices believing they were following the will of God? Even sadder is how often those people are portrayed as heroes and examples of the perfect believer. Islamic suicide bombers are a great example of this. Consider the amount of faith required to strap on an explosive vest and kill yourself and others in the name of your God. I would contend that it's impossible to have any more faith than that. Ah, but great is their reward in heaven—or so they were told.

Job is supposedly one of the oldest book in the Bible and is a good example of someone who believed unwaveringly in God. To the best of his abilities, Job followed what he believed God wanted him to do. He even offered daily sacrifices just in case one of his ten children had committed a sin and forgot to repent of it. Yet despite all of his faith and efforts, all of his children were killed, all of his cattle (which was essentially money at the time) were stolen or killed, as well as almost all of the servants that watched over them—all because, according to the story, God had basically made a bet with Satan and was proving a point.

The point of Job's story is that God is God and we are mere mortals who, quite frankly, have no right to complain or even ask for an explanation. At the end of the story, Job has rebuilt his cattle to double the number he had to begin with and his wife has given him ten more children. Therefore, believers claim God has repaid him for his faithfulness. But if you actually consider all of the people involved and the consequences they paid because of God's bet, it becomes quite hard to see any justice or reward. To me, it's one of a great many illustrations of God's seemingly callous disregard for human life and suffering.

What about all of the cattle herders that were killed? How were they repaid? How were their families repaid for the loss of a husband, father, or son? What about the ten children? How did they get repaid? Are ten new children really a replacement for ten children you raised to adulthood? Are people replaceable like tires on a car?

As the parents and others mentioned above learned, what the Bible says and what actually happens are two different things. For me, it's absolutely unbelievable that, in spite of the completely undeniable fact that the result they experienced is not at all what the Bible says would happen, many of them continue to believe!

Imagine if I told you that if you planted M&M candies in some dirt mixed with sugar and then "watered" it with milk, it would grow a bush that would produce M&Ms. You would think I was just crazy; but imagine if I really insisted that it was true and it just required a little bit of faith—comparatively, no more than a mustard seed. In fact, if you truly believe what the Bible says, I can state unequivocally that, if you have the faith of a mustard seed, you *can* plant an M&M and grow a bush that would produce M&Ms.

1. *"With man this is impossible, but **with God all things are possible**."* (Matthew 19:26, ESV)

2. *"For **nothing will be impossible with God**."* (Luke 1:37)

3. *"With man it is impossible, but not with God. For **all things are possible with God**."* (Mark 10:27, ESV)

4. *"For truly, I say to you, if you have faith like a grain of mustard seed, you will say to this mountain, move from here to there, and it will move, and **nothing will be impossible for you**."* (Matthew 17:20, ESV)

5. *"And I will do whatever you ask in my name, so that the Father may be glorified in the Son. **You may ask me for anything in my name, and I will do it.**"* (John 14:13–14)

Now I realize that you're going to object that Jesus wasn't talking about planting M&M bushes. Although I would argue that "anything" or "all things" truly means *anything*, for the sake of argument I'll accept your objection. So instead, let's apply those verses to a terminally ill person.

I personally know of a case where many people were praying for the healing of a young, devout Christian girl. She had gotten married less than a year earlier and had recently been delighted to find out she was pregnant with her first child. Then she was given the devastating diagnosis that she had cancer. She was in her mid-twenties, raised in a Christian home, ate a vegan diet, exercised regularly, didn't smoke or drink, didn't do drugs, and served the Lord to the best of her abilities.

The family and church rallied around her and began praying for God to heal her. They spread the news and organized prayer vigils at certain times where well over a thousand people were simultaneously praying for her healing. Apparently, none of those people had the faith of a mustard seed. In fact, even the combined faith of over a thousand people apparently didn't add up to the faith of a mustard seed. She spent her last few weeks making little cards of encouragement, faith, and hope which she gave to other patients in the hospital and sent to everyone she knew. Not because she was trying to win God's favor, but just because she was an amazing young woman and understood their pain and struggles. Sadly, there was no healing.

The same scenario is repeated thousands of times every day all over the world. Currently (the year 2023), about 167,000 people die worldwide every single day. While many of those are older people or those that have abused their bodies with drugs, alcohol or poor diets, plenty are people still in the prime of their life and even children that certainly haven't done anything to "deserve" to die. Yet all the prayers, anointings, and other rituals can't get one of those "promises" fulfilled.

If over a thousand believers, all agreeing and praying for the same thing, can't prompt the all-powerful, kind, loving heavenly Father to fulfill the promises He made in the Bible and heal one of his followers, do you really think He's going to help you find your car keys? Inspire someone to give you a job? Aid your investments? Protect your loved ones? Save your marriage?

CHAPTER 3

THE INERRANT WORD OF GOD

The Bible is presented to believers as the absolute Word of God, a rock-solid foundation upon which to build their faith and beliefs. Unfortunately, if you actually research the history of the Bible and its various sources and translations, you will find that what we read today is far less certain and authoritative than its proponents would have us believe. From the meaning of the original words, to the authors of the ancient writings, there is a great deal of debate and differing opinions, even among the scholars that believe it is in fact the inspired Word of God. We see this today in the multitude of sects, denominations, and religions that all claim the Bible as the basis of their beliefs.

Although I had Bible class and church school lessons on the traditional Bible stories, it wasn't until I was nineteen that I really started reading the Bible simply to find out what it actually said. It was an eye-opener. The first and most shocking thing I found was that it didn't say many of the things that I'd been told it said. While I read many of the texts I'd heard used to support various beliefs, I found that many of them, when taken in context, did not mean what I'd been told they meant. Furthermore, there were several texts that plainly contradicted some of the things I'd been taught and which, for some odd reason, I'd never heard quoted in church.

Over time I came to realize a truth that was stated quite well by Mark Twain:

> In religion and politics people's beliefs and convictions are in almost every case gotten second-hand, and without examination, from authorities who have not themselves examined the questions at issue but have taken them second-hand from other non-examiners, whose opinions about them were not worth a brass farthing.[15]

---

15 Mark Twain, *The Autobiography of Mark Twain, Including Chapters Now Published for the First Time* (New York: Harper & Brothers, 1959), 369.

I finally realized that, obviously, the church and my teachers were mistaken in some of their beliefs. For me, that was a shocking realization.

Trying to tell other believers about the errors was the next shocking experience. While I wasn't surprised that they were naturally skeptical of my claims, it was the defensiveness, anger, and utter refusal to accept what the Bible actually said—even when it was plainly shown to them in black and white—that I didn't expect. I *thought* people wanted to know the truth. What I learned was that most people generally don't want to hear anything that is contrary to their beliefs. Nobody likes being wrong, but they especially don't like being wrong about their religious beliefs.

I think the reason it is so disturbing to them is because it threatens their belief that they are going to the happy hunting grounds when they die. I mean, if they were to accept that they were actually wrong about a fundamental belief that they had learned in church, what else might they, and the church, be wrong about? Thinking that the church could possibly be wrong ranks nigh unto blasphemy for most true believers. Thinking that the church could possibly be wrong about the requirements for being accepted into eternal life, well, now that can flat-out make you weak in the knees.

I learned over time that it was best not to drop too much truth onto someone all at once. The human mind and its belief systems just can't deal with it. Just as we learn to read, write, and spell over time by starting with letters and the simplest and smallest words first, likewise it's generally best to start with small doses of less earth-shattering truths first.

Unfortunately, I don't have that luxury here. My best suggestion is, read only as much as you can deal with and verify that the evidence I give is in fact correct. Then ponder that evidence for a while until you can modify your belief system to handle it, or reject it. You don't have to accept that it means what I say or imply it means. That's the beauty of free choice... You can believe whatever you want. But don't deceive yourself. Rejecting things that are true, just because you don't happen to like them, or because they force you to change, is not the path to wisdom. It *is* the path to cowardly, willful ignorance and the pain and suffering that will inevitably bring.

As I studied the Bible more, I learned that you can't always believe what it says. It turns out that various translators have made quite a few "mistakes" in translation. There are many ancient copies of a lot of the books in the Bible. Unfortunately, many of the copies don't exactly match, and there often isn't an obvious "original" version. Translators have to decide which version of a particular text is most likely the correct one. Consequently, just as in the ancient copies themselves, different versions of the Bible have, or don't have, verses or parts of verses contained in other versions—another shocking revelation. I had been taught that the Bible was the **inerrant** word of God. God said what He meant and meant what He said.

Alas, it turns out that what we read isn't necessarily what was actually said. For example, I learned that one of the Ten Commandments (the Holiest of the Holy Rules) stated, "Thou shalt not kill." Lo and behold, it turns out that what was actually said was, "Thou shalt not commit murder."

At first blush, many people seem to think both of those mean the same thing, but they are profoundly mistaken. The difference between killing and murdering is a matter of *justification*. Killing is the *justified* ending of a life. Murder is the *unjustified* ending of a life. The truth of this becomes blatantly clear by simply reading the rest of the laws that God gave Moses for the people to live by. Death (killing) was the punishment God gave for quite a range of crimes, and it was the duty of the people to carry out those executions.

It would be rather inconsistent, not to mention hypocritical, for God to give a commandment forbidding killing and then continue on and make rules that required killing. But in this case, the pieces all fall neatly into place as soon as you realize that God never outlawed killing in the first place; He just outlawed *unjustified* killing (murder).

Amazing! Just a minor inaccuracy in the translation of a single word and yet the difference in the resulting beliefs caused by that one little word is profound indeed. How many Christians are opposed to the death penalty because they, quite mistakenly, believe that God said "Thou shalt not kill." In fact, they can even prove it in black and white in their preferred version of the Bible. It is a disturbing realization that, if there is one mistake in translation (and a mistake in a *very* fundamental belief), there are probably more.

How many more? And what impact will they have on other beliefs we may have? There are many more examples of Biblical translation inaccuracies you can read about in various books. Many newer Bible translations will give you the reasons that words or complete verses were changed from those used in older translations.

More disturbing than translation errors are those cases when the same story in different parts of the Bible is translated correctly, yet they blatantly disagree with each other. For example, the story about King David counting the fighting men among the people. The story is told in two different books of the Bible: 2 Samuel 24 and 1 Chronicles 21. In the 2 Samuel version, it says the Lord (God) incited and *told* David to number the people. In the 1 Chronicles version, it says it was Satan that incited David to number the people. Furthermore, the number of fighting men listed in the two versions is not the same. If the exact same story can have such irreconcilable differences, even when translated correctly, how can the Bible possibly be considered *inerrant*? By the way, don't take my word for it, read the two chapters yourself.

Another example is the presumably accidental division of the last two verses of 2 Chronicles with the first three verses of Ezra. The first two and a half verses of Ezra are word-for-word duplicates of the last two in 2 Chronicles. In fact, the last verse in 2 Chronicles stops right in the middle of a sentence which is completed in the third verse of Ezra. Oops, some scribe made an error in the *inerrant* word of God. Again, look it up for yourself.

Numbers are hard to argue with. In the second chapter of the book of Ezra, there is a long list of the Israelites who returned from Babylon to Jerusalem. The list begins with the following words:

> Now these are the children of the province that went up out of the captivity, of those which had been carried away, whom Nebuchadnezzar the king of Babylon had carried away unto Babylon, and came again unto Jerusalem and Judah, every one unto his city.

In the seventh chapter of Nehemiah, there is a copy of the very same list. In the preface to the list, Nehemiah seems to have simply copied Ezra. He begins, starting in the middle of verse five:

> And I found a register of the genealogy of them which came up at the first, and found written therein, These are the children of the province that went up out of the captivity, of those which had been carried away, whom Nebuchadnezzar the king of Babylon had carried away unto Babylon, and came again unto Jerusalem and Judah, every one unto his city. (vv. 5–6)

Exactly the same list. No one can argue that this was some other list. In each account, there follows a list of families that came out of Babylon, with the number of persons belonging to them. But in transcribing them, Nehemiah made many errors.

FAMILY	EZRA	NEHEMIAH
Parosh	2,172	2,172
Shephatiah	372	372
Arah	**775**	**652**
Pahath-Moab, etc.	**2,812**	**2,818**
Elam	1,254	1,254
Zattu	**945**	**845**
Zaccai	760	760
Bani	**642**	**648**
Bebai	**623**	**628**
Azgad	**1,222**	**2,322**
Adonikam	**666**	**667**
Bigvai	**2,056**	**2,067**
Adin	**454**	**655**
Ater	98	98
Bezai	**323**	**324**
Jorah (Hariph)	112	112
Hashum	**223**	**328**
Gibbar (Gideon)	95	95
Beth-lehem and Netophah	**179**	**188**
Anathoth	128	128
Azmaveth	42	42
Kirjath-arim, etc.	743	743
Ramah and Gabah	621	621
Michmas	122	122
Bethel and Ai	**223**	**123**
Nebo	52	52
Magbish	**156**	

FAMILY	EZRA	NEHEMIAH
Elam	1,254	1,254
Harim	320	320
Lod, Hadid, and Ono	**725**	**721**
Jericho	345	345
Senaah	**3,630**	**3,930**
Jedaiah	973	973
Immer	1,052	1,052
Pashur	1,247	1,247
Harim	1,017	1,017
Jeshua, etc.	74	74
Asaph	**128**	**148**
Shallum, etc.	**139**	**138**
The Nethinim, etc.	392	392
Delaiah, etc.	**652**	**642**
Servants	7,337	7,337
Singers	**200**	**245**

Out of forty-three groups in the list, there are twenty errors. That's not what *inerrant* looks like. And this is just one example.

Ezra and Nehemiah agree on the number of domestic animals there were, but they disagree in the oblations. Ezra says they gave 61,000 drams of gold, 5,000 pounds of silver, and 100 priestly garments. But Nehemiah says that they gave 41,000 drams of gold, 4,200 pounds of silver, and 597 priestly garments.

Yet people insist that there is not one error in the Bible. They try to blame it on copyists or translators, but that is still an error. If God is going to provide His Perfect Word to humankind and have them write it down, He certainly wouldn't let it be corrupted by translators, would He?

There are many numerical errors in the Bible. Here are a few more just to further make my point.

When did Ahaziah son of Jehoram begin his reign in Judah?

> In the eleventh year of Joram the son of Ahab began Ahaziah to reign over Judah. (2 Kings 9:29)

> In the twelfth year of Joram the son of Ahab king of Israel did Ahaziah the son of Jehoram king of Judah began to reign. (2 Kings 8:25)

How old was Jehoiachin when he began to reign?

> Jehoiachin was eight years old when he began to reign. (2 Chronicles 36:9)

> Jehoiachin was eighteen years old when he began to reign. (2 Kings 24:8)

How long did Jotham reign in Jerusalem?

Sixteen years. (2 Kings 15:33)

At least twenty years. (2 Kings 15:30)

How old was Ahaziah when he began to reign?

Twenty-two years old. (2 Kings 8:26)

Forty-two years old. (2 Chronicles 22:2)

How long did Omri reign?

From the 31st to the 38th year of Asa's reign. That equals 7 years, yet Omri is said to have reigned twelve years—an impossibility. (1 Kings 16:23, 28–29)

How much gold was brought to Solomon from Ophir?

420 talents of gold. (1 Kings 9:28)

450 talents of gold. (2 Chronicles 8:18)

How many stalls did Solomon have for his horses?

4,000 stalls. (2 Chronicles 9:25)

40,000 stalls. (1 Kings 4:26)

How long did Gad tell David he was to suffer famine?

   Three years. (1 Chronicles 21:11–12)

   Seven years. (2 Samuel 24:13)

How many horsemen did David take with him from Hadadezer?

   700 horsemen. (2 Samuel 8:4)

   7,000 horsemen. (1 Chronicles 18:4)

According to Genesis, Noah was five hundred years old when he begat Shem (Genesis 5:32). Noah was six hundred years old when the Flood waters were on the earth (Genesis 7:6). Shem was one hundred years old when he begat Arphaxad, two years after the Flood (Genesis 11:10). This is a mistake. If Shem begat Arphaxad two years after the Flood, then he should have been 102 years old.

The author of Matthew recounts all the generations from Abraham to Jesus. He lists that there are forty-one names, including Abraham and Jesus. Then, he goes on to say that there are *fourteen* generations from Abraham to David, *fourteen* generations from David until the "carrying away into Babylon," and then *fourteen* generations from there to Christ. This is in Matthew 1:17. Three times fourteen is *forty-two*, not *forty-one*.

I've found that most believers *really* don't like to consider questions like these. They prefer to sweep them under the rug, telling themselves, for example, that the difference between kill and murder is only a minor difference, not really all that important. Or that, if it's wrong to murder, it must be even better not to kill at all! A human being's ability to bullshit (sorry, I can't think of a more accurate word) themselves (and others) is most remarkable, eclipsed perhaps only by their utter lack of logic. For Christian believers, Jesus said, "*Know* the truth, and it will set you free," yet most of them tend to go through life as if their motto is "Ignorance is bliss." They like to call it "faith."

In his book *Mere Christianity* (which should be a must-read for any Christian), C. S. Lewis discusses this type of "faith." He calls it "blind faith." As he says, it's lazy, disgusting, willful ignorance, and absolutely no different than superstition. As far as these "believers" are concerned, someone told them something was true, and that's as far as their logic and reasoning goes. If the Pope/Priest/Pastor/Prophet/Elder/Whoever said it, then that's all they need to believe it. We've all heard the old saying, "If it was good enough for my forefathers, it's good enough for me." That's some very poor logic.

There are multiple books and websites that document contradictory statements in the Bible. One book is *The Age of Reason* by Thomas Paine, a founding father of the United States. Read *The Age of Reason* or search "Biblical Contradictions" on the internet. Look at the examples given and then actually look up the Bible verses and verify for yourself whether they are contradictory or not. You will find it a troubling but enlightening experience. Go ahead. If you tend to believe the Bible is at least a fairly accurate translation of God's words, take the time to do this research and then come back. I'll wait.

Another enlightening exercise is to get a version of the Bible containing Strong's numbers. Those numbers are used to reference the original Hebrew or Greek word that was translated into the particular word you see in whatever version of the Bible you're using. What's interesting is looking at all of the *other* words that the original word *could* have been translated into. The meaning of many verses can be changed dramatically just by choosing a different, yet valid, translation of the original word.

In Hebrew, like most ancient languages, most words had multiple meanings. Many words have *a lot* of different meanings. In English, we can often determine the correct meaning of a word by the way it is used in a sentence. Likewise, biblical translators can often determine the appropriate meaning by the other words in the sentence. On the other hand, it seems they just as often translated them based on the religious beliefs that existed, or that they wanted to promote, at the time.

The oldest texts date back to somewhere between 1400 and 1500 BC. The rest of the Old Testament books were written between then and the last book, the book of Malachi, which was written about 435 BC. The oldest translation of the Hebrew texts is known as the Septuagint, which was created beginning around 280 BC. It was a translation of Hebrew into Greek due to an order of the King of Egypt, Ptolemy II. Even at that time, there were multiple versions of the Hebrew texts the Septuagint translators had to choose between. While many had mostly minor differences, some had many significant differences.

It's important to realize that when the Septuagint was being created, the oldest Hebrew writings were already more than a thousand years old. There had been extensive cultural, linguistic, and religious changes over that time. To help put it in perspective, consider, for example, the cultural, language, and religious differences between today and our European ancestors of a thousand years ago. Try reading an English book written even five hundred years ago. It's almost a foreign language, and the meanings of many words have changed significantly since then. In addition, to really be able to understand, you often need to understand the environment, circumstances, and issues of the time it was written in.

There were several other translations made between 300 BC and 1400 AD. Starting around 1400 AD, the Bible began to be translated into English. The most famous of these translations is known as the King James Version. For many people, this is the one and only "true" version of the Bible. If they only knew...

In the last 150 years, there has been a virtual explosion of translations. Many of them would be more accurately described as a loose interpretation rather than an actual translation. It's also important to realize that modern translations have been filtered through two thousand years of changing Christian theology. This is especially problematic with the Old Testament Hebrew books since they were written long before Christianity came along.

All of this makes it rather difficult to determine exactly what the original meaning of the text was.

Once we realize that the Bible is not in fact inerrant, the problem becomes how are we supposed to know what the truth is? How do we know that the Bible has been translated correctly? How do we know it hasn't been modified, added to, or subtracted from? How do we know that the people who wrote the various books we call the Bible were actually telling the truth?

In religion, the typical method of proving something is to make a statement of supposed truth, and then use what is written in the Bible or some other book written by the founder or leaders of the religion to "prove" that the statement is in fact true. In the discipline of logic, this is known as "circular reasoning." Using a book as "proof" first requires that you believe the book's author knows the truth. In other words, you first have to believe in the author before you can believe in statements made by the author. So, for an example of circular reasoning, when a Mormon tells you "a truth" and then uses a book written by Joseph Smith (the founder of Mormonism) to "prove" the truth, they are using circular reasoning. How can a "truth" be *proven* by referring to the writings of the person that "discovered" (or made up) the "truth" in the first place? If the author gives some external, objective method of proving the "truth," then there might be something you can research or examine to determine whether the "truth" is true or not. But just because the author states that it's true in his book, is no proof at all. Furthermore, you would have to *believe in* the author if the only evidence presented is that he (or she) said (or wrote) it. Do you *know* the author? Have you met the author?

In the case of the Bible, supposedly God personally wrote the Ten Commandments and inspired other people to write the rest of it. Stop and think about this for a moment. The only reason anyone would believe in the Christian God is because they believe in the Bible. But the only reason anyone would believe in the Bible is because they believe it was "written" (inspired) by God. Again, this is circular reasoning. Which comes first, the belief in God or the belief in the book written by God?

In fact, the situation gets even worse. For thousands of years now, no one has been able to find the two stone tablets on which God supposedly wrote those Ten Commandments. All we have now is a book written by a man named Moses that claims that God did in fact write Ten Commandments on two tablets of stone. Consequently, to believe in the Christian God, we are now in the awkward position of first having to believe in a *man*! Not one of us has any personal experience with Moses. How can you believe in a book written by someone you've never met and who has been dead for thousands of years?

On a slight side note, stop and think about the biblical story of the writing of the Ten Commandments. Moses goes up on a mountaintop that God has come down to (landed on?) and spends forty days up there while God writes the Ten Commandments. This is the same God that, according to the same Bible, created the entire universe—the earth and every living thing in it—in seven days (seven evenings and mornings)! How could it possibly take such a God forty days to merely write Ten Commandments on two tablets of stone? Not only did it take Him forty days, but after Moses broke the original two tablets, it took Him another forty days to rewrite them.

Now stop and think...how long do you think it would take Moses to carve out two tablets of stone and write Ten Commandments on them? Just asking. Remember, Moses was raised as a prince in Egypt, and if there's anything Egypt is known for, it's the amazing stonework.

Let's finish this chapter by looking at the Bible's history as we know it today. The word "Bible" means "books." The Bible is a *collection* of books that were written over fifteen to sixteen centuries by dozens of authors. When most Protestant people think of the Bible, they think of the King James Version or one of the myriad alternate translations of the same sixty-six books. But multiple other versions of the Bible contain more books than the King James Version. The Catholic Bible contains seventy-three books. The Ethiopian Orthodox Bible contains eighty-one books. Over the last two thousand years, there have been several "Bibles" with differing numbers of books.

Many of the extra books in the Catholic and Ethiopian "Bibles" come from a collection of books known as the Apocrypha, which, according to Merriam-Webster, are books included in the Greek Septuagint and Latin Vulgate but excluded from the officially accepted Jewish and Protestant versions of the Old Testament, early Christian writings not included in the New Testament, and other writings or chapters of biblical books which were excluded from the "official" versions. Even the number of books in the Apocrypha varies between denominations and nationalities.

The point is that a fair number of Hebrew and Greek religious writings were considered for inclusion in our modern Bibles but were rejected. The Old Testament books have two main versions: the Septuagint and the Masoretic Text. The two versions differ not only in the number of books but also in the number of added or removed verses and changes in the wording of various verses. The Masoretic Text is the source for the official Hebrew Bible and was the main source used for the Old Testament of the King James Version.

So, who decided which books should be included in our modern English Bibles? Well, as with most everything related to the Bible, it involved many people over an extended period. The one thing all of these people had in common is that they were all members of the Catholic Church. This is the church that evolved out of the followers of Jesus and his disciples and that many people, myself included, consider to be the most evil organization that has ever existed on the face of the earth in all of recorded history. When it comes to slaughtering innocent people, the Catholic Church makes Hitler, Stalin, and Mao tse-Tung look like mere amateurs.

I need to take a minute to give a little background on the Catholic Church. But first, let me be clear here. When I say the Catholic Church, I'm referring to the organization and its leadership, not most of the millions of Catholic believers that just aren't aware of the facts about their church. The Catholic Church **caused** what we call today "the Dark Ages." Beginning in the latter half of the fourth century AD, they began destroying books, education, and all other forms of knowledge everywhere they had control. They made Latin the "official" language of church writings so that the "common" people couldn't read them and then went on to forbid the "common" people from having most books, *even the Bible*! Over the next several centuries, using church laws, wars, and murder, the church quite effectively kept the general public illiterate and almost absolutely ignorant. Ignorant people are easy to control. The greatest threat to tyrants is knowledge.

It wasn't until the Reformation (beginning with Martin Luther's Ninety-five Theses) and the ultimate breaking of the Church's control when French troops commanded by Napoleon Bonaparte defeated the Church's army, occupied the Papal States, and took the Pope prisoner in 1798 that the western world began to recover from the centuries of ignorance the Catholic Church had caused. The world had to relearn the math, astronomy, and science that the Greeks knew before Christianity started. No one knows how many "heretics" the Church slaughtered during the Dark Ages, but it was many millions. The Reformation alone started a century of warfare between the Church and the Protestants (the protestors). Just during the Thirty Years War, which was part of that century of warfare, around eight million people were killed. During the French Wars of Religion, over three million were killed. You need to keep in mind that the total population was much lower then and that those millions of people killed amounted to significant percentages of the total population. It has been estimated that Germany lost up to 40 percent of its population just during the Thirty Years War.

The Thirty Years War ended in peace treaties signed in 1648, known as the Peace of Westphalia. Two of the main tenets of the treaties were that each King or Prince was free to choose the religion of their territory, and Christians of all denominations were guaranteed the right to practice their particular faith. The treaties also stripped Ferdinand III of his power as the Holy Roman Emperor. That prompted Pope Innocent X to declare it "null, void, invalid, iniquitous, unjust, damnable, reprobate, inane, empty of meaning and effect for all time."[16] Fortunately, the European Kings, both Catholic and Protestant, completely ignored his declaration.

Sorry for the digression, but now back to the concept of the "inerrant" Word of God. Do some research on the translations of various words from the original Hebrew or Greek. For example, what we read as the singular "God" in our modern versions of the Old Testament, unless it's referring to a specific deity, was generally the plural word "Gods" in the original Hebrew; i.e., there were multiple Gods. And it wasn't referring to the Father, Son, and Holy Ghost. The "Trinity" is a concept that

---

16 Holy Roman Empire Association, "The Peace of Westphalia—1648," accessed September 19, 2024, https://www.holyromanempireassociation.com/peace-of-westphalia.html.

was simply made up by the Catholics. Contrary to what Christian preachers tell you, the Old Testament doesn't mention Jesus or the Holy Ghost.

The Hebrew word most commonly translated as "God" in modern Bibles is Elohim, pronounced as El-o-heem. Elohim is actually the *plural* form of the word "El," which is the correct word for the singular form of "God." In English we generally add the letter "s" to signify the plural form of a word. In Hebrew the "im" ending signifies plural. So, in an accurate translation, Elohim *should* be translated as "Gods." The same word is also translated as Goddess, rulers, divine, divine being, exceedingly, godly, great, judges, and mighty in different verses. Look it up in Strong's Concordance (it shows all the words that the original Hebrew or Greek *could* be translated as). Also check out the original word translated as "kill" in the King James Version of the Ten Commandments. (It should have been translated as "murder.")

Most Christians think of the word "God" as the *name* of the creator, the God of Israel and the supreme being, but it's not. Yahweh or Jehovah is the *name* of the God of Israel. God is actually a word like "human" or "cat" or "bird." It refers to a *type* of being. We have various titles for certain people such as President, Doctor, Ambassador, General, Captain, etc., but in all those cases, the person is still a "human," and they each have their own name. Likewise, the Gods may be referred to by different titles such as Lord, Angel, etc., perhaps based on the task they are performing, but they are all "gods," and they each have their own name. Just like humans.

The reason we generally see Elohim translated as "God" in modern Bibles is because when they were translating the Bible in the 16th century, and even to this day, the dogma of a single supreme being that created and ruled over the entire universe and every living thing in it had been firmly established by the Catholic Church for many centuries. So, in most cases, to translate it correctly as "Gods" would have been considered heresy, and at that time heresy could get you burned at the stake, or worse. Furthermore, all of the men doing the translation were Christians and, consequently, the idea of multiple Gods would have disagreed with their personal beliefs as well, regardless of what the Hebrew texts actually said.

But *if* they translated it correctly, we could read the first part of Genesis as:

> In the beginning the Gods created the sky and the land. And the land was without form, and void (empty); and darkness was upon the face of the deep. And the wind of the Gods moved over the

surface of the waters. And the Gods said, "Let there be light"; and there was light. And the Gods saw the light, that it was good; and the Gods divided the light from the darkness. And the Gods called the light Day, and the darkness they called Night. And the evening and the morning were the first day.

I know most Christian readers will react to the translation I used above as if it were heresy and think I'm trying to deceive them. But if you look up each of the words in Strong's Concordance that are different from what you're used to hearing, you will find that it is a perfectly legitimate translation; and I believe it's far more accurate. The choice of the biblical translators to use "God" instead of the correct word "Gods," which is what the Hebrew text actually says, is the real deception. Since translating it accurately wouldn't have supported the dogma of Christianity, they **purposely** mistranslated it. Stop and consider that for a few minutes.

They also chose to use "Heaven" and "Earth" rather than the just as legitimate (and more rational) "sky" and "land" for the same reason.

As long as we're looking at the first part of Genesis, let me point out another illogical point of Christian dogma. We are told that the word "void" meant there was *nothing* there at all until "God" created the Earth. But that doesn't make any sense. It clearly states there was "darkness upon the face of the deep." And what is the "face of the deep"? The ocean, the water that covered the entire earth (the earth was a water world before the Gods began modifying it). In fact, it adds a supporting statement to that concept with the words that "the wind of the Gods moved over the surface of the waters." If there was *nothing* there at all, what are the waters that it's talking about? Where did they come from? The "waters" and the "face of the deep" are both referring to the same thing: the ocean. And again, where did it come from? Nowhere does it say that "God" *first* created the "deep" and the "waters." It's clear that they were already there when "God" began his acts of creation. But that doesn't fit the dogma—which is why that's not what you are taught.

As long as you're looking at Strong's Concordance, browse through it a little, and you'll notice that **most** of the original Hebrew or Greek words have many different English words that they could have been translated into. I've noticed the same thing with most ancient languages. Apparently, they had much smaller vocabularies than we do today. Consequently, they used the same word to mean many different things. While we have some words like that ("file" for one example), it seems **most** of their words had different meanings depending on how they used them.

If you look at some verses and the other words that could have been used, you'll find that the meaning of the verse changes rather dramatically depending on which of the valid translation words you choose. It's also interesting to look at how the translators chose different English words in different verses even though the original word is exactly the same. Sometimes that makes sense because of how the word is used. But often there's no apparent reason for using a different word. Different translators with different opinions maybe? Choosing the word that best makes the verse conform to the translators' beliefs maybe?

Let's go back to the topic of who decided which of the books should be included in our modern English Bibles. Again, it was the Catholic Church. I find it less than reassuring that the murderous Catholic Church, with some modifications by the Reformers (mainly the removal of the books of the Apocrypha), happens to be the organization that decided which writings were "holy" and which were not. And which English words were chosen during translation. I also find it strange that God, being as particular about numbers as He is, would have "inspired" the creators of His Holy Word to create a book consisting of 66 books. From the Biblical perspective, the number 6 represents imperfection, man, and evil. 666 is the number of the Beast of Revelation. The number 7 represents perfection,

God, and sacredness. So why are there 66 books rather than 77? Just coincidence?

As I've made clear from the beginning, this book is intended to motivate and point you in the right direction to find the extensive amount of detailed evidence assembled by many other authors regarding the points I bring up. Those authors have spent years researching, organizing, documenting, and then presenting that evidence in well-written books and articles.

As just one example, I'm including an article written by Sophiee Saguy. Sophiee happens to practice Judaism. The main point of her writings is that Christianity is *not* Judaism plus Jesus. The practitioners of Judaism do not believe in Jesus or the New Testament. Sophiee explains why and provides a lot of evidence of how the New Testament is has been cobbled together over the last two thousand years. The following is one of her articles reprinted here with her permission (emphasis mine).

CAN YOU TRUST THE CHRISTIAN BIBLE FOR ACCURACY?

My intent here is not bash the Christian bible, but it is important for religious people to take a look at the accuracy of the T'nach (Jewish Bible) as well as the accuracy of the Christian bibles of today. I will discuss the methods Jews have used for thousands of years to maintain Torah accuracy (and they are amazingly the same as even ancient archeological discoveries attest) to the Christian bibles which have more differences than they have similarities.

If you are a Christian, are you really following the teachings of Jesus? It is impossible (with what we know today) to **prove** that Jesus even existed. Don't get upset—I am not saying Jesus is fictional, I'm simply saying it is impossible to **prove** one way or the other, let alone know what Jesus might have said based on the current Christian bible.

Why do I say "current Christian bible"? Isn't it two thousand years old?

Nope, not hardly. Most modern Christian bibles actually date to the twentieth century. Eberhard Nestle produced the first edition of the Novum Testamentum Graece in 1898. The Textus Receptus was first edited in 1516 by the Catholic Reformer Desiderius Erasmus. The King James translation was primarily from the Textus Receptus although they did "glean" about three hundred-plus variances from other Greek sources. Most modern Christian translations are based on an edition of the Nestle-Aland/United Bible Society (NA/UBS) text (a variation of the Nestle text).

Committees decide which text to use gleaned from various sources. The King James translators did this, and the KJV varies from the Textus Receptus in 287 places. The King James was actually based more on the third edition of the Greek New Testament issued by Stephanus (of Paris) than from the Textus Receptus.

The Novum Testamentum Graece on which the Nestle is based was also decided by committee who gleaned through a large number of manuscripts to decide which texts they thought were more "true." Most modern Christian translations are based on the Novum Testamentum (Nestle). Wikipedia has an article listing many of the differences between them. Wikipedia also has an article entitled "Textual variants in the New Testament" which states "John Mill's 1707 Greek New Testament was estimated to contain some 30,000 variants in its accompanying textual apparatus which was based on nearly 100 [Greek] manuscripts. Eberhard Nestle estimated this number in 1897 as 150,000–200,000 variants. Bart D. Ehrman has estimated that there are between 200,000–400,000 variants based on 5,700 Greek and 10,000 Latin manuscripts, various other ancient translations, and quotations by the Church Fathers," and in 2014 Eldon J. Epp raised the estimate as high as 750,000. Still, Epp says that there is "no reliable estimate of the total number of variants found in our extant witnesses."

There is no Greek manuscript that agrees exactly with either the Textus Receptus or the Nestle... Both of them combine text from various earlier Greek sources. Men on these committees decide which to pick and choose, and which to reject. This is why there is no Christian Bible of today that one can point to as the "truth" of the early Christians, let alone what Jesus might have said if he lived and is quoted properly...(the earliest papyri date to, at the earliest, fifty years after Jesus's death and possibly quite a bit later...how many quotes do you think are remembered fifty years after the fact?).

This just goes to show that the Christians have a serious problem when it comes to piecing together Bibles. The early Greek papyri contradicted each other to an enormous amount. "What do survive are copies of the copies some 5,366 of them in the Greek language alone, that date from the second century down to the sixteenth. Strikingly, with the exception of the smallest fragments, no two of these copies are exactly alike in all their particulars. No one knows how many differences, or variant readings, occur among the surviving witnesses, but they must number in the hundreds of thousands." (The Orthodox Corruption of Scripture: The Effect of Early Christological Controversies on the Text of the New Testament. New York: Oxford University Press, 1993, page 27).

The Nestle is very close to the text of Westcott-Hort which in turn is taken from the Codex Vaticanus (fourth century). There are variations of the Nestle as well! The Gospels "do not go back to the first century of the Christian era" (Catholic Encyclopedia, Farley ed., vol. vi, p. 137, pp. 655–6). "The earliest of the extant manuscripts [of the New Testament], it is true, do not date back beyond the middle of the fourth century (CE)" (Catholic Encyclopedia, op. cit., pp. 656–7).

"The differences among the manuscripts have become great, either through the negligence of some copyists or through the perverse audacity of others; they either neglect to check over what they have transcribed, or, in the process of checking, they make additions or deletions as they please." Origen (circa 235 CE) early church father in "Commentary on Matthew." Codex Sinaticus and Vaticanus both date to the fourth century CE. Not only are Sinaiticus and Vaticanus not word-for-word representations of today's Christian Bible, but they don't even include the same books in the Christian Bible canon as today's RCC and Protestant version. Sinaiticus adds Hermas and Barnabas. Vaticanus omits 1–2 Timothy, Titus, James, 1–2 Peter, 1–3 John, Jude, and Revelation. The inclusion or omission of these works do change the *Christian Bible* theology significantly.

Vaticanus is missing over 1,491 words and clauses. It is also missing everything after Hebrews 9:14.

Sinaticus does not, but it also has lots of gaps—due probably to careless scribes who left out ten to forty words in various places. Just sloppy. Then there is the Codex Alexandrinus—likewise from the fifth century. It is missing forty pages—including Matthew 1:1–25:6, John 6:50–8:52, and II Corinthians 4:13–12:6. Now we come to the Codes Bezae, from the fifth or sixth century. It has the gospels (lots of omissions) and the Acts (missing from 29:22 onwards) in Greek and Latin...

Codex Sinaticus omits the following verses (which are in Codex Vaticanus):

- Matthew 24:35—"Heaven and earth shall pass away, but my words shall not pass away"
- Luke 10:32
- Luke 17:35
- John 9:38

- John 16:15
- John 21:25
- I Corinthians 13:2

Next note that Vaticainus leaves out the following verses while Sinaiticus keeps them:

- Matthew 12:47
- Luke 23:17

By the way. this verse is left out in B and the NASB, NIV but it is in Sinaiticus and the Majority of all Greek texts "For of necessity he must release one unto them at the feast."

Again, B omits Luke 23:34 "Then said Jesus, Father, forgive them; for they know not what they do" while it is retained in Sinaiticus and this time kept in the NASB, NIV. Go figure.

In the gospels alone, both Vaticainus and Sinaticus leave out the following verses.

- Matthew 17:21
- Matthew 18:11
- Matthew 23:17
- Mark 7:16
- Mark 9:44
- Mark 46
- Mark 11:26

- Mark 15:28
- Luke 9:55-56
- Luke 17:36
- Luke 23:17
- John 5:4

The NASB of 1972 omitted these verses, but in 1977 put them back [in brackets]. The NIV continues to omit these verses entirely.

Just to help you out a little bit, here is a list of scriptures in the Christian Bible that have been archeologically proven to be forgeries, which is to say, they do not appear in the oldest **complete** manuscripts:

- Matt. 5:23 without a cause
- Matt. 6:13 For thine is the Kingdom, and the power, and the glory, for ever. Amen.
- Matt. 6:25 or what ye shall drink*
- Matt. 16:2 When it is evening, ye say, it will be fair weather: for the sky is red.
- Matt. 16:3 This entire verse
- Matt. 17:21 and fasting
- Matt. 18:12 into the mountains
- Matt. 20:7 and whatsoever is right, that shall ye receive
- Matt. 22:13 and take him away
- Matt. 23:35 son of Barachias*
- Matt. 24:10 and shall hate one another*

- Matt. 24:31 sound of a*
- Matt. 24:41 women shall be
- Matt. 25:6 cometh
- Matt. 27:52 and the graves were opened*
- Matt. 27:53 and went*
- Matt. 28:19 therefore
- Mark 4:37 so that it was now full*
- Mark 6:51 beyond measure and wondered
- Mark 7:8 For as the washing of pots and cups: and many other such like things as ye do
- Mark 7:14 unto me every one of you
- Mark 9:24 with tears
- Mark 9:29 and fasting
- Mark 9:44 This entire verse
- Mark 9:45 into the fire that shall never be quenched
- Mark 9:46 This entire verse
- Mark 9:47 fire
- Mark 9:49 and every sacrifice shall be salted with salt
- Mark 10:24 for them that trust in riches
- Mark 10:30 houses and brethren and sisters and mothers and children and lands with persecutions*
- Mark 14:30 twice*
- Mark 14:68 and the @#%$ crew
- Mark 14:72 the second time* twice*
- Mark 16:9-20 All these verses
- Luke 2:40 in spirit
- Luke 8:45 and sayest thou, Who touched me?

- Luke 16:16 and every man presseth into it
- Luke 17:12 which stood afar off*
- Luke17:35 women
- Luke 18:11 with himself*
- Luke 22:43 This entire verse
- Luke 22:44 This entire verse
- Luke 22:68 me, nor let me go
- Luke 23:5 teaching*
- Luke 23:34 Then said Jesus, Father forgive them; for they know not what they do
- Luke 24:42 and of an honeycomb
- John 1:25 asked him, and*
- John 3:13 which is in heaven
- John 4:9 for the Jews have no dealings with the Samaritans
- John 5:3 waiting for the moving of the water
- John 5:4 This entire verse
- John 5:25 and now is*
- John 8:1-11 all these verses
- John 8:59 going through the midst of them and so passed by
- John 16:16 because I go to the Father
- John 19:23 and also his coat*
- John 21:25 This entire verse
- Acts 6:3 Holy Ghost and (should read "spirit of")
- Acts 6:8 faith (should read "grace")
- Acts 8:37 This entire verse
- Acts 9:31 churches (should read "church") were (should read "was")
- Acts 15:32 and confirmed them*

- Acts 18:5 pressed in the spirit (should read "earnestly occupied with the Word")
- Acts 18:21 I must by all means keep this feast that cometh in Jerusalem: but
- Rom. 3:22 and upon all
- Rom. 6:12 it in
- Rom. 7:6 that being dead (should read "being dead to that")
- Rom. 8:26 for us
- Rom. 11:6 But if it be of works, then it is no more grace; otherwise work is no more work
- Rom. 14:6 and he that regardeth not the day, to the Lord he doth not regard it
- 1 Cor. 2:1 testimony (should read "mystery")
- 1 Cor. 6:20 and in your spirit, which are God's
- 1 Cor. 7:5 fasting and
- 1 Cor. 10:28 for the earth is the Lord's and the fulness thereof
- 1 Cor. 15:24 cometh
- 2 Cor. 4:14 by (should read "with")
- Gal. 3:1 that ye should not obey the truth
- Gal. 3:17 in Christ
- Gal. 5:19 adultery
- Gal. 5:21 murders
- Eph. 5:9 Spirit (should read "light")
- Eph. 5:30 of his flesh, and of his bones
- 2 Thess. 2:9 Even him
- 1 Tim. 3:16 God (should read "who")*
- 1 Tim. 4:12 in spirit*
- 1 Tim. 6:5 from such withdraw thyself*

- 2 Tim. 3:3 without natural affection*
- Heb. 12:18 mount that might be touched and that burned with fire (should read "fire that might be touched and burned")*
- Heb. 12:20 or thrust through with a dart*
- James 5:16 Confess your faults (should read "Therefore confess your sins")*
- 1 Pet. 2:5 spiritual (before the word "sacrifices")
- 1 Pet. 3:8 courteous (should read "humble")
- 2 Pet. 1:1 God and our (should read "our Lord and")*
- 1 John 3:16 of God
- 1 John 5:7 in heaven, the Father, the Word and the Holy Ghost: and these three are one
- 1 John 5:8 And there are three that bear witness in earth
- 1 John 5:13 and that ye may believe on the name of the Son of God
- Rev. 1:17 unto me, Fear not*
- Rev. 2:22 their (should read "her")*
- Rev. 5:3 neither under the earth*
- Rev. 5:9 us (omitted by the Alexandrian Ms., one of the three oldest Mss. known)
- Rev. 5:10 us (should read "them") we (should read "they")
- Rev. 5:13 and under the earth*
- Rev. 6:2 to conquer (should read "he conquered")*
- Rev. 9:4 neither any green thing*
- Rev. 9:13 the four horns of*

- Rev. 10:6 and the sea, and the things which are therein*
- Rev. 11:17 and art to come*
- Rev. 12:12 inhabiters of* of (before the words "the sea")
- Rev. 14:5 before the throne of God*
- Rev. 14:12 here are they*
- Rev. 16:5 and shalt be (should read "the holy")*
- Rev. 16:7 another out of*
- Rev. 16:11 and their sores* of their deeds*
- Rev. 16:17 from the throne*
- Rev. 18:22 of whatsoever craft he be* and the stone of a millstone shall be heard no more at all in thee*
- Rev. 20:5 But the rest of the dead lived not again until the thousand years were finished*
- Rev. 21:24 of them which are saved* and honor*
- Rev. 21:26 and honor*
- Rev. 22:3 more*

The ones marked with an asterisk (*) do not appear in the Codex Sinaiticus. The ones without (*) do not appear, as they are written in contemporary Christian Bibles, in either the Codex Sinaiticus, or the Codex Vaticanus. These are the two oldest complete, or nearly complete Greek Manuscripts of the Christian Bible. Granted there are portions of the C.V. that are missing.

All credit to and written by Sophiee Saguy.

(For more of Sophiee's writings, including 365 well-written repudiations of "messianic prophecies" in the Old Testament, go to her website: https://nojesus4jews.weebly.com.)

As we end this chapter, let's review. Is the Bible the "inerrant" Word of God as many Christian denominations like to claim? Not even close. Words were both purposely and accidentally translated incorrectly. Verses were added and removed, and sometimes accidentally moved to a completely different book of the Bible. Plenty of irreconcilable contradictions can be proven just by using the Bible itself. They are **irreconcilable** because there's no way they can both be true. One **has** to be wrong. Or in other words, in error.

I just gave a few examples of the differences in the original manuscripts and irreconcilable contradictions that have been documented. But as I said before, I'm not going to rewrite all of the excellent work done by other authors. If you want to know the truth, you're going to have to spend some time and effort researching it. I told you of Thomas Paine's book, *The Age of Reason*. You can read it in an evening. Read it. Another book worth reading is *Is It God's Word?* written by Joseph Wheless in 1926. You can find it at the following web address:

https://archive.org/details/isitgodsword0000jose or just do an internet search using the title and author's name. Also, do an internet search for "Biblical Contradictions." And then, as I've said before, don't take the author's word for it, read the Bible verses they present for yourself, and you decide. Do they agree or not?

CHAPTER 4

TWO GODS, TWO BOOKS, TWO RELIGIONS

Before getting into the differences between the Old and New Testaments, I would like to point out a couple of things. First the name "Jesus" is the Greek version of "Yeshua," which was the actual Hebrew name of the main character of the New Testament. Yeshua, when converted to English, is Joshua. I don't know why when the original translators were translating the Bible to English they didn't bother to translate Yeshua to the more correct Joshua, but they didn't. Most of the time I will use the original name Yeshua. You can mentally convert that to Jesus whenever you see it.

Second, I'd like to point out that the New Testament is all about Yeshua, which the New Testament declares to be the Messiah. The New Testament (and all of Christianity) claims that Yeshua is the fulfillment of "all those Old Testament prophecies" that say that God would send a Messiah to free His people, crush their enemies, exalt Israel over all other nations, and rule the world from Jerusalem. But let's take a minute to look at "all those Old Testament prophecies" of the Messiah.

It turns out that the word "Messiah" is only used twice in the entire Old Testament (using the King James Version). Both times in the book of Daniel (9:25 and 9:26). According to Strong's Concordance, the word translated in Daniel as "Messiah" is actually used 38 times in the Old Testament. In **every single one** of the other thirty-six verses that use the word, it is translated as "anointed" and refers to a king, a priest, or some other specifically ordained person that was particularly chosen by God. So why is it translated as Messiah in Daniel? This is one of those cases where the translators chose a different English word than **every other case** where the exact same Hebrew word was used. Why would they do this? Because it helps make the (incorrect) case that Daniel's prophecies were predictions of Yeshua, which was the prevailing belief when the Bible was translated into English.

Very few of those thirty-six verses use the term in reference to anyone in the future. Of the few that do, when read in context, the only way you could come to the conclusion that they are referring to Yeshua is if you already believed Yeshua is the Messiah and use a lot of creative imagination and interpretation. In many of the newer translations, such as the NIV, ASM, ESM, NRSV, etc., the word Messiah ***never*** appears in the Old Testament at all. In those versions, the word in the two verses of Daniel is correctly translated as "anointed," which is consistent with every other time it is used.

The fact is, there is no belief, concept, or specific teaching anywhere in the Old Testament of a coming Messiah, a son of God sent to die on a cross to save the world. Furthermore, there is absolutely zero evidence that the Israelites prior to Yeshua's time ever believed any such thing. It is a story completely created in the New Testament. Likewise, the concept of going to heaven or hell when we die, and even the concept of hell itself, are also creations of the New Testament. I'll talk more about the "messianic prophecies" later.

Another creation of the New Testament is the idea of the Devil or Satan, the supreme evil being that is the enemy of God and humans. It was a concept that developed over time. Originally, God, or the Gods, was seen as the cause of most everything, good and bad. They sent the seasons, the rain, tornadoes, locusts, floods, volcanoes, etc. In fact, Yahweh states in Isaiah 45:7, *"I form the light, and create darkness: I make peace, and create evil: I the Lord do all these things."* He neither needed a Devil to accomplish what He wanted, nor someone to blame for punishments the people didn't like. Read the story of Exodus when Moses was trying to get Pharaoh to let the Hebrews go. The Bible clearly states, repeatedly, that God hardened Pharaoh's heart so he would not let the people go. Notice that it's not "the Devil" hardening Pharaoh's heart. If there was a Devil capable of battling with God, then God wouldn't really be God, would he? But that's never the picture we get from the Old Testament. God took the credit, or blame, for everything. But as the idea of a kind heavenly Father was developed, it became necessary to have someone else to blame for all the evil in the world. So evil became personified and was named the Devil.

The word "Satan" as used in the Old Testament simply meant "adversary or accuser or opponent." Most significantly, it is **not** used to refer to a supreme evil being. The word was applied to various humans, including David when he was living with the Philistines (Samuel 29:4), Hadad the Edomite (1 Kings 11:14), Rezon the son of Eliada (1 Kings 11:23 and 25), and one of God's angels blocking Balaam's donkey (Numbers 22:22). Look up the English word "adversary" used in each of those verses in Strong's Concordance and you will see that the Hebrew word was "satan." Christians point to the book of Job as proof that there is a being named Satan. But if you look at the original Hebrew texts, you will find that the being referred to simply as "Satan" in our modern English Bibles was actually referred to as "the satan." In other words, the word satan was used as a description or title of the angel's *job* as the adversary or accuser, not his or her *name*. Note that "the satan" in Job was completely subordinate to God. Just another one of God's servants. There are a lot of religious ideas, concepts, and beliefs that are completely based on the New Testament alone and simply don't exist in the Old Testament. A supreme evil being called the Devil or Satan is one of them.

As most people know, the Bible is divided into two sections: the Old and New Testaments. From those two sections, we get two different religions: Judaism and Christianity, both of which *claim* to believe in the same God. Yahweh (YHWH, Jehovah, or whatever pronunciation you prefer) is the God of Judaism which is based on the Old Testament alone. Yeshua is the God of Christianity which is based on the New Testament. Judaism doesn't consider the New Testament to be scripture and consequently doesn't accept that Yeshua was the Son of Yahweh, or the Messiah. Meanwhile, the various Christian faiths can't agree on whether Yeshua was Yahweh in human form or the son of Yahweh, or both. Jews don't believe Yeshua was the Son of Yahweh, or the Messiah, and consequently don't believe in the New Testament at all. Christians will tell you they believe in the entire Bible. But that's not true. Christianity is completely based on Yeshua and the New Testament and pretty much ignores most of the practices and rules of the Old Testament.

The differences between Judaism and Christianity are quite significant. Practitioners of Judaism observe (more or less) the rules, requirements, and holy days of the Old Testament. They don't observe the holidays and other rituals associated with Yeshua, such as Christmas, Easter, or Communion—at least not as part of their religious practice. Christians, on the other hand, don't observe the holy days of the Old Testament nor, for the most part, most of its rules and regulations. They explain that Yeshua "fulfilled" the Old Testament, and consequently, they no longer have to live by those rules and regulations. It's interesting to note that in the book of Isaiah (66:18–23), it states that in the New Earth people from all nations will come to worship God "from one New Moon to another and from one Sabbath to another." In other words, the Old Testament New Moon holy day will be observed in the New Earth. So it's rather odd that Christians don't bother to observe it now.

It's quite interesting to compare the God of the Old Testament with the "Father" God of the New Testament. They are as different as night and day. Completely different personalities. Like Jekyll and Hyde. In His own words, the God Yahweh of the Old Testament was a "jealous" God. The first of the Ten Commandments He gave to Moses was, *"Thou shalt have no other Gods before me."* While He often claimed to be the greatest of the Gods (most Gods do), it is very clear from His own statements that He acknowledged the existence of other Gods—which is the entire reason for the first commandment. Yahweh also made it quite clear, repeatedly, that He was the God of Abraham, Isaac, Jacob (whose name was changed to Israel) and the nation of Israel. It's important to note that He **didn't** claim to be the God of Egypt, Syria, Babylon, or any other nation. In fact, the Bible clearly identifies and names the Gods of many other nations. Yahweh was quite clear in differentiating between **His people** (the Jews) and those that were **not His people** (everyone else).

This God was directly involved in ruling His people. He communicated directly with many of them: Abraham (He even had lunch with Abraham), Moses, Daniel, Ezekiel, and many others according to the Bible. He often executed His punishments directly as well. He was a rather strict deity that didn't suffer fools gladly. He generally didn't have a lot of patience, and His forgiveness was rather hit or miss. He refused to forgive the people over twenty years old when they didn't charge into Canaan on the exact day He wanted them to. Even though they repented and were willing to go the very next day (see Deuteronomy 1:19–45). Nope, God had already decided they were never going to set foot in the promised land and wouldn't forgive them. He also refused to forgive King Saul when he disobeyed (see Deuteronomy 1:19–45). Esau too was denied forgiveness though he sought it with tears (see Hebrews 12:16–17).

Yahweh's standard form of punishment was killing those that had annoyed Him (drowned the entire planet once) or, more often, killing a large number of other people that didn't actually have anything to do with the offense that made Him mad (see the story of David numbering the fighting men of Israel in 1 Chronicles 21 for just one example).

One of the most striking differences between the Old and New Testament Gods is the fate of the people they loved and assisted. Most of the people in the Old Testament that God liked became national leaders or powerful, rich, influential people or great warriors that slaughtered large numbers of Israel's enemies against great odds. His people were "winners." He made them "winners." He protected them and killed their enemies. Men like

Abraham, Joseph, Moses, Daniel, Elijah, Samuel, David, and many others. He was a God of victories!

This is the God that gave Moses the Ten Commandments on Mount Sinai. This is an important point to remember. We'll come back to it later.

The "Father" God of the New Testament (which supposedly is the same Yahweh), on the other hand, doesn't really do much. He's the "kind, loving, heavenly Father" that Christianity teaches. He's extremely patient, loves everyone, is infinitely forgiving, and almost never executes any punishment. Unfortunately, His special people don't become wealthy, powerful leaders. He doesn't protect them. He doesn't kill their enemies. He doesn't lead them into battle and give them victory. Instead, He tells them to not defend themselves. To love and submit to their enemies. To quietly and willingly go to their own execution. He is the God of sheep being led to the slaughter—the exact opposite of the God of the Old Testament. Kinda odd isn't it?

The truth is, Yahweh isn't really the God of the New Testament; Yeshua is. Christians proclaim that He **is** God, the Word of God made flesh (John 1), or at least *"one with God"* (John 10:30). And they worship him **as** God. Yeshua himself told his disciples that *"he that has seen me has seen the Father"*

(John 14:9). It makes me wonder. If Yeshua was Yahweh, then who was he praying to? Who was the one who *"sent him"* (John 8:29)? Why did he tell Mary after his resurrection not to cling to him because he had *"not yet ascended to the Father"* (John 20:17)? A whole lot of verses make absolutely no sense whatsoever if you try to claim that Yeshua and Yahweh were the same person. And the Trinity concept (which is nothing more than a Catholic fabrication) just makes things worse.

In the Old Testament, Yahweh states that he never changes (Malachi 3:6). But if you believe He is the Father God of the New Testament, then you would have to conclude that He does change. A lot. In the Sermon on the Mount, Yeshua starts off by saying that *"until heaven and earth pass away, not the smallest letter or stroke shall pass from the Law until all is accomplished."* Then He goes on and repeatedly quotes laws of the Old Testament and follows that by saying, *"But I tell you"* (Matthew 5) and either completely reverses it as in the case of an *"eye for eye and tooth for tooth"* to *"turn the other cheek"* or, as in the case of adultery, greatly expands it so that even looking at a woman with lust is the same as committing adultery (Matthew 5:27–28).

Side note: Actually, the word translated as "lust" there is the same word translated as "covet" in a number of other verses including the tenth Commandment. In addition, the word translated as "woman" in Matthew is the same word translated as "wife" in the tenth Commandment. The point I'm making here is that it **could** be interpreted that what Yeshua was actually stating was that violating the tenth Commandment by coveting your neighbors' wife was essentially the same as violating the seventh Commandment against adultery. But that's not how it reads in our modern Bibles.

Let's consider what is today called the "Mosaic Law" or "Law of Moses." The term is generally used to refer to the first five books of the Bible. But among Christians, it is usually used to mean all of the rules and regulations (laws) that Moses told the people of Israel to follow **other than the Ten Commandments**. Christians make this distinction because it is blatantly obvious that they don't abide by those laws. In fact, it's often the difference in which of those "Mosaic Laws" that a particular Christian denomination chooses to follow that separates them from the other Christian denominations. But regardless of which Christian denomination you look at, none of them come close to following the "Mosaic Law." If they did, they would be practicing Judaism, which they don't.

The question here is, **Why don't they follow the Mosaic Law**? Yeshua followed it. His twelve disciples followed it, and they taught the new Christians to follow it as well. Paul, the guy that wrote the majority of the New Testament, on the other hand, didn't follow it and argued that it was no longer relevant. In fact, whether Christians had to follow the Mosaic Laws was **the** big point of disagreement between Yeshua's disciples and Paul when he visited Jerusalem. In Acts 21:20, James and the other "elders" pointed out that thousands of Jews had become believers and *"all of them are zealous for the law."* They then go on to point out in Acts 21:21 that these believers had heard that Paul taught *"all the Jews who are among the Gentiles to forsake Moses, telling them not to circumcise their children or observe the customs"* (i.e., the law).

These are just a couple of verses in the New Testament that make it clear there were already two different versions of Christianity being taught during the disciples' lifetimes. One version, taught by Yeshua's disciples, included following the Mosaic laws and customs, and a second version taught by Paul ignored the Mosaic laws and customs. How can this be? As we read above, Yahweh claims he never changes (Malachi 3:6) and Yeshua said *"Do not think that I have come to abolish the Law or the Prophets; I have **not** come to abolish them but to fulfill them. For truly I tell you, until heaven and earth disappear, not the smallest letter, not the least stroke of a pen, will by any means disappear* *from the Law until **everything** is accomplished."* (Matthew 5:17–18; emphasis mine)

Even today, based on the large number of biblical prophecies that have yet to occur, no one can honestly claim that *"everything is accomplished."* It should also be blatantly obvious that heaven and earth have not disappeared, so, according to Yeshua's statement above, *"not the smallest letter, not the least stroke of a pen, will by any means disappear from the Law."* Many modern Christian leaders try to claim that Yeshua was just referring to the Ten Commandments, but it's perfectly clear that is not what he was talking about if you read the verse in context.

Ultimately, Paul's version of Christianity won and became the basic version that all Christian denominations follow today. Paul argued that Yeshua "fulfilled" the Mosaic Law and thereby eliminated the need to follow it. It's important to note that you can't support that idea from any of Yeshua's or his twelve disciples' teachings or from anywhere else in the Bible other than Paul's writings. By Yeshua's time, the Pharisees and Sadducees had added a lot of rules and regulations to the laws given by Moses (as authorities love to do) that Yeshua denounced, even though he told his followers to do everything the religious leaders told them to do (Matthew 23:3). But Paul didn't agree with that. Not only did he teach the Gentiles that the Pharisees' and Sadducees' rules and regulations didn't need to be observed, he completely threw the baby out with the bathwater. **Both** the Mosaic Law and everything that had been added to it.

It's also important to note here that the Jews aren't the ones that Christianized the world. While Yeshua obviously had a number of followers while he was alive (enough for the religious leaders of his time to consider him a threat), after his death the vast majority of Jews did not convert to the new Christian religion, nor did they consider Yeshua a fulfillment of any Old Testament prophecy. While there are some Christian Jews today, the vast majority of the Jewish people don't believe in or accept the New Testament as scripture. It was Paul's "gentile" followers that created the Catholic church and spread Christianity throughout the world. And that version of Christianity was Paul's version.

So where exactly did Paul get his version of the gospel? According to Paul, it was given to him through revelation directly by the resurrected Yeshua (Galatians 1:11–12). In another verse, he also refers to revelations as one of the sources of his theology (Ephesians 3:3–4). Although Paul says the revelations were from Yeshua, how would he know? He never personally met Yeshua, so he's just taking the word of whoever is speaking to him in his revelations. How do **we** know that it was Yeshua? And if it was, why was Yeshua teaching Paul something different than what he himself taught his disciples when he was alive?

In Acts 19:21, it says Paul *"purposed in the Spirit"* to go to Jerusalem and then to Rome. In Acts 23:11, it says that the "Lord" told Paul he must also be a witness for him in Rome. What Spirit and Lord are these? Most Christian theologians agree that it was the Holy Spirit and the resurrected Yeshua. On his way to Jerusalem, Paul spent seven days in Tyre. While he was there, the believers *"through the Spirit…kept telling Paul not to go up to Jerusalem"* (Acts 21:4). What Spirit? Again, Christians state it was the Holy Spirit, and I would agree that is certainly what the Bible would seem to indicate. So, the Holy Spirit is telling Paul one thing and then telling the other Christians the exact opposite? Seems a bit strange, doesn't it?

But Paul was undeterred. After leaving Tyre, he stopped by Ptolemais and then went to Caesarea where he stayed for many days. While he was there, a prophet came from Judea and said that if Paul went to Jerusalem, he would be arrested and turned over to Gentiles (Acts 21:11). When the believers there heard it, they, as well as Paul's traveling companions, urged him not to go to Jerusalem. Again, this is a message coming from the Holy Spirit and being given to multiple people warning Paul not to go where he's planning to go.

In Romans 1:13, Paul states that many times he had intended to go to Rome *"but have been prevented from doing so until now."* Prevented by whom? In many other writings of Paul, he repeatedly claims to have been informed by, led by, and worked with the Holy Spirit, including in Acts 16:6–7, where it states that the Holy Spirit prevented him from going to Asia and then shortly after that the Spirit would not let him enter Bithynia. It seems pretty clear that it was the Holy Spirit that had been preventing Paul from going to Rome.

Let's think about this for a minute. Supposedly the Holy Spirit has guided Paul into going to Jerusalem and Rome. But then, by the urgings of this same Holy Spirit, many believers tell Paul not to go to Jerusalem or Rome. Is this how Yahweh and the Holy Spirit work? Tell one person one thing and then tell other people the exact opposite? Does that make any sense? Why would the Holy Spirit be impressing other people to warn Paul not to go to Jerusalem? Why not just tell Paul directly since, supposedly, this same Holy Spirit had been leading Paul for years? The only logical conclusion is that either Paul was not listening to the Holy Spirit or that the Holy Spirit guiding Paul simply wasn't the same Holy Spirit impressing all of those other believers.

Could this be why Paul's version of the Gospel eliminates the Mosaic Law and is different from what Yeshua and his disciples taught? Does it make any sense that Yahweh (who never changes) would give Moses a set of laws, rules, and regulations and then have his supposed son Yeshua teach his disciples a new set of beliefs (the messianic gospel) and then turn around and throw out everything he told Moses and give Paul another new set of beliefs (the messianic gospel with the Mosaic laws removed)? Or is it more likely that Yeshua and Paul just came up with their own ideas and did their best to convince people to adopt their new beliefs?

Since I don't want to get lost in the weeds, the point is, whether we credit Yeshua, Peter, Paul, James, John, or Mary, the religion they started is a very different religion than the one based on the Old Testament. Different rules, different rituals, different holy days, and, quite frankly, different Gods. The Old Testament is focused almost entirely on God trying to get the people of Israel to obey the laws, rules, and regulations He gave to Moses so He could "bless" them and make them a mighty nation. Although it does promise earthly rewards for being a loyal follower of Yahweh, significantly it is **not** focused on the individual's personal "salvation" or their reward of eternal life, which is the **entire** focus of the New Testament. For the individual, the Old Testament is primarily focused on the here and now. The New Testament adopts a victim mentality and basically assumes life in this world is going to be miserable. So instead, it focuses on being "saved" so you can enjoy the wonderful joys of heaven after you leave this world. A rather profound philosophical contrast.

The truth is, the Old and New Testaments don't belong in the same book. The only reason we find them in the same book is because the Catholic Church combined them to create the "Bible" and to try to give the new religion of Christianity some legitimacy as just a new and improved version of Judaism. It's much easier to sell a new deal (or New Covenant) if you can link it to the old deal (or Old Covenant). Even better if you claim that the new deal isn't really new, that it was in fact the original plan all along! And God was just waiting for the "right time" to bring his only begotten son into the world to reveal the true plan!

Let's go back to that first Commandment: *"You will have no other Gods before me."* If Yeshua is not in fact the same being as Yahweh, and I would argue that he isn't, then worshiping Yeshua would in fact be putting another God (even if it is

God's son) before Him. Given the history of how Yahweh deals with His enemies, both foreign and domestic, how do you think He might treat those that violate His first Commandment and substitute some other God for Himself? Considering how he historically treated "his people" when they sinned and followed other Gods, maybe the persecution that Christians have both suffered and inflicted on others over the last two millennia is Yahweh's attempts to try and enlighten someone.

CHAPTER 5

NEW TESTAMENT PROBLEMS

There are a lot of "issues" with the New Testament besides the fact that, as I pointed out in the last chapter, it is an entirely different religion than the one of the Old Testament.

The first issue is: who actually wrote the books we now call the New Testament? There is a lot of controversy and debate on this issue. While I'm not going to get into all of the details, I do suggest you do some research on the subject. The main point I want to make is that when and by whom these books were written is far from certain. What is fairly certain is that many of them (if not all) were **not** written by the personal disciple of Yeshua that they are named after. The dedication to Theophilus in the first four verses of Luke makes it clear that the author is **not** Luke the disciple. Specifically, the author states that the account of the events was *"handed on to **us**"* (i.e., including himself) from those who were eyewitnesses (i.e., **not** including himself). In other words, these were stories about Yeshua and the disciples that had been told and passed around for some time. It's also well known that there were several other "gospels" about Yeshua that **didn't** get included in the official version of the New Testament.

You would think, or at least I would think, that if God was sending His very own son to explain to the entire world what God expects of them and that believing in His son was the **only** method of achieving eternal life, He would have made sure that at least a couple of those twelve disciples were scribes that kept an **accurate** record of the events and teachings of Yeshua. Better yet, it seems Yeshua himself should have written down the things God wanted us to know like Moses did. If you accept that Yeshua was who the New Testament claims he was, then there couldn't be **anything in all of history** more important than making sure there was a thorough, accurate record of the "new covenant" that God was making with humanity.

Alas, somehow that little detail was overlooked by the God of infinite wisdom that knows everything from the beginning to the end. Not only did He overlook it, but Yeshua himself apparently didn't think it was important either. Apparently, humanity is supposed to figure out the most important issue of their life from a mishmash of differing stories and philosophies written down by who knows who after they had been passed around by word of mouth for years.

Exactly how long it was between the crucifixion and the writing of the books is, not surprisingly, also a matter of debate. Almost all scholars agree that the oldest New Testament writings were written about one hundred years after Yeshua was executed. Some Christian scholars claim fifty years—still a long time.

We all know what happens as a story gets told and retold, which can partially help explain why the first four books (Matthew, Mark, Luke, and John) have a number of detailed differences that raise questions about their authenticity. While Matthew, Mark, and Luke seem to have a common source, John is significantly different in style and content from the other three. It doesn't have a lot of the material found in the others, including some rather important events, such as the temptation of Yeshua, the transfiguration, the Last Supper, the casting out of demons, the Sermon on the Mount, and the Lord's Prayer. Interestingly, John doesn't include any of the parables either.

On the other hand, John is the **exclusive** source for other stories about Yeshua. Only in John do we find the story of Lazarus—which I find odd. While not the only person Yeshua raised from the dead, Lazarus was the only one that had been dead for four days. It would seem this would have been the most impressive and important of all the miracles Yeshua performed. Yet only John mentions it? The other gospel writers apparently didn't find it important enough to include in their version of events. John is also the almost exclusive source for the claim that Yeshua was in fact Yahweh himself. While verses in other books can be "interpreted" (twisted) into meaning that, only John states it unequivocally. And repeatedly. Another odd oversight by the other writers, since one of the biggest questions of the twelve disciples themselves was trying to understand exactly who Yeshua was.

It is generally agreed that John was written later than the other three gospels. It makes me think of the truism "the tale grows taller on down the line." Stories tend to get bigger and "better" the more they are told. In the other three gospels, we have a story of the Son of God, his teachings, his life and death. But by the time John writes it, he's no longer just the Son of God, he is God Himself. Creator of the universe. The first created of all things. A much "bigger and better" story than the others told.

Thirteen of the twenty-three books of the New Testament were supposedly written by Paul (formerly known as Saul). Although there is some debate on that, it's fairly well agreed that at least seven of the thirteen were definitely written by Paul. It's strange that half of the New Testament would have been written by a single person, one that never actually met Yeshua and wasn't one of his special twelve disciples. In fact, he was not taught by, nor a member of, the disciples of Yeshua nor did he accept that they had any higher calling or claim to authority than himself. Paul basically claims that he was appointed by Yeshua himself after he had ascended to heaven. From there, Paul apparently came up with his own theology of Christianity. And he happens to be the only New Testament writer that made the Gentiles (non-Jews) the exclusive target of his ministry. On a side note, it's also strange that even under the "new covenant" of Christianity, God's rules, regulations, and requirements are different for Jews versus Gentiles. Peter and Paul hammered out some of those differences in one of Paul's visits to Jerusalem (see Acts 15).

We can still see this dichotomy of beliefs in the various denominations of Christianity today. They pick and choose which rules and regulations they think they are required to observe and then argue about them. When they want to "prove" they don't have to observe certain Old Testament requirements, they point to Paul's writings. When they want to "prove" that they do have to observe certain Old Testament requirements, they point to the Old Testament, Yeshua, and his disciples' teachings. Both positions can be equally defended using the exact same Bible. To me, this is just more evidence that Christianity is a man-made religion. While I would agree that there was a man named Yeshua who may have believed he was the Son of God and managed to get himself killed by the religious leaders of his time, most of the rest of the stories about him and his life are just that—stories.

If you really want some entertaining stories about Yeshua, you should read the Gospel of Thomas, contained in the Apocrypha. It contains many stories of Yeshua's childhood and the miracles he performed as a child. While it's impossible to read it and not believe it's anything other than complete fantasy, I would point out that it's not really any more fantastic than the stories included in the accepted version of the Bible. Christians are just familiar with the magical events in the official version of the New Testament, so they don't seem like complete fantasy. They are just part of the "faith" they adopted when they became believers.

Or they were taught them from childhood, so they seem "natural."

Besides the totally magical aspect of giving sight to the blind and curing people that had been crippled from birth, there are other issues related to these suddenly restored abilities that never occur in the Bible stories. Beginning in 1960, modern science has been able to restore the sight of a number of people that have gone blind. Other than the very few cases where the patient had not been blind for very long (less than a year), there were significant issues for the people that had their sight restored. For many, the first few moments were quite traumatic and confusing. Their brains didn't know how to process the new visual input. The ability to recognize objects and to be able to tell how near or far away an object is will take anywhere from a week to a few months to relearn. To get to the point of being able to see what we would consider "normally" takes years. Apparently, it takes the human brain a fair amount of time to learn how to interpret and understand what we see. Yet in the Biblical stories, the people whose eyes were suddenly healed experience none of those issues.

As we know with people that become paraplegic today, all of the muscles associated with standing, walking, running, and jumping will wither away. For those that were born crippled, those muscles never develop in the first place. If we could restore the nerve connections to those muscles, it would take a fair amount of work to build up the muscles and learn how to control them. Consider how long it takes a child to learn how to walk. First, they start by simply standing while their muscles grow stronger and they begin to learn some basic balancing skills. Then they begin taking a few steps, and over a number of weeks and months, they learn how to walk and run.

But in the Bible stories, the healed people go from having been completely lame for years to instantly walking, running, and jumping around, including those who had been lame from birth. So not only was the nerve issue that kept them from being able to walk fixed, but their muscles were also instantly built up and their brains were instantly trained (programmed?) to know how to balance, walk, and jump. Stop and think about that for a minute, especially the brain aspect.

While I understand that if you believe in a God with unlimited magical abilities, there's no difficulty in believing that He can just magically fix everything. But when it comes to modifying (healing, training, or whatever you want to call it) the neural connections in the brain that are created by experiences that give us the ability to see and walk, you really need to consider what that implies. Basically, it implies that God can just "download," change, and overwrite information in a person's brain whenever He wants.

That would also be the only logical conclusion when you think about the story of God "confusing" the people's languages at the Tower of Babel (see Genesis 11:1–9). He didn't just "confuse" them; He removed the knowledge (memories, neural connections, brain pathways) of whatever shared language they had all spoken up until then and replaced it with multiple languages (when did He make those up?) and all of the memories, neural connections, pathways, and tongue and mouth "muscle memory" to enable them to speak, hear, and understand their new language. Are humans nothing more than computers that God can reprogram at will? And if we are, what's the point in killing the ones that annoy Him when He could just reprogram them to not do those annoying things?

Before someone claims that it's because He has to allow us our "freedom of choice," it's quite obvious He didn't care about the freedom of choice of the people at the Tower of Babel. They had agreed to work together and build a city. But, because God didn't like what they were doing, He just overrode their choice by reprogramming them with different languages. This is also a fundamental problem with the Christian concept of "freedom of choice." You can't really call it "freedom of choice" when the only choice is to bow down and worship me or die. Interestingly, even Yeshua refused to do that when the Devil tempted him and chose to die.

Another issue we see with the New Testament is that of "cherry picking." The practice of finding verses, or portions of verses, and then using them completely out of context to support a favorite theory. And apparently the practice of "revisionist history" started long before today. Matthew 1:22–23 quotes the prophecy of Isaiah Chapter 7 regarding the virgin birth of a son that was to be named Immanuel as evidence that Yeshua's virgin birth was the fulfillment of an Old Testament prophecy.

Unfortunately, if you actually read the prophecy in Isaiah 7, it is blatantly clear that it was to be a sign for Ahaz the reigning king of Judah at that time. The main point of the prophecy was that the two kingdoms threatening to attack Judah at that time, Israel (called Ephraim in Isaiah) and Assyria, would both be laid waste **before the child Immanuel was old enough to "reject the wrong and choose the right"**; i.e., twelve years old. It would make no sense whatsoever that God would give King Ahaz a "sign" (proof) that wouldn't occur until centuries later when Yeshua was born and Ahaz was long dead. Furthermore, Yeshua wasn't named

Immanuel. The only reason Yeshua is referred to as Immanuel today is because of Matthew's claim that Yeshua was the fulfillment of that prophecy. It's a totally irrational and false claim.

Likewise, the unknown author of Hebrews' description of Moses's hasty departure from Egypt after killing an Egyptian is complete revisionist history. According to Exodus 2:14, when Moses found out that people knew he had killed the Egyptian, *"he was afraid"* (NIV). Remember that Exodus was supposedly written by Moses himself; i.e., Moses himself is telling everyone that he fled Egypt because he was afraid. But the writer of Hebrews claims the exact opposite: *"By faith he left Egypt, not fearing the king's anger"* (Hebrews 11:27).

Professional apologists try to claim that this verse refers to when Moses led the people of Israel out of Egypt. But that explanation falls flat for a number of reasons, the best being that when the people of Israel left, the king of Egypt had told Moses to take them and leave. In other words, there was absolutely no reason for Moses to be afraid of that king. He was simply doing what the king had told him to do. Also, it's important to note that the king of Egypt at the time of the Exodus was not the same king ruling Egypt when Moses ran after committing murder (see Exodus 2:23). Again, since this king didn't know Moses, there wouldn't be any reason for Moses to be afraid of him, nor any reason for the writer of Hebrews to mention that he left, *"not fearing the king's anger."*

The above are just a couple examples of the types of problems found in the New Testament. With a little research and reading, you can find many more of those types of issues. But now let's look at what I believe is the biggest issue with the New Testament: Yeshua's own failed predictions (prophecies) about his imminent return to judge and rule the earth. First, let's look at exactly what Yeshua said.

> For the Son of Man is going to come in the glory of His Father with His angels, and will then repay every man according to his deeds. Truly I say to you, there are **some of those who are standing here who will not taste death until they see the Son of Man coming in His kingdom**. (Matthew 16:27–28; emphasis added)

> Behold, I have told you in advance. So if they say to you, 'Behold, He is in the wilderness,' do not go out, or, 'Behold, He is in the inner rooms,' do not believe them. For just as the lightning comes from the east and flashes even to the west, so will the coming of the Son of Man be. Wherever the corpse is, there the vultures will gather.

But immediately after the tribulation of those days the sun will be darkened, and the moon will not give its light, and the stars will fall from the sky, and the powers of the heavens will be shaken. And then the sign of the Son of Man will appear in the sky, and then all the tribes of the earth will mourn, and they will see the Son of Man coming on the clouds of the sky with power and great glory. And He will send forth His angels with a great trumpet and they will gather together His elect from the four winds, from one end of the sky to the other.

Now learn the parable from the fig tree: when its branch has already become tender and puts forth its leaves, you know that summer is near; so, you too, when you see all these things, recognize that He is near, right at the door. Truly I say to you, **this generation will not pass away until all these things take place**. (Matthew 24:25–34; emphasis added)

Then they will see the Son of Man coming in clouds with great power and glory. And then He will send forth the angels, and will gather together His elect from the four winds, from the farthest end of the earth to the farthest end of heaven. Now learn the parable from the fig tree: when its branch has already become tender and puts forth its leaves, you know that summer is near. Even so, you too, when you see these things happening, recognize that He is near, right at the door. Truly I say to you, **this generation will not pass away until all these things take place**... (Mark 13:26–30; emphasis added)

Then they will see the Son of Man coming in a cloud with power and great glory. But when these things begin to take place, straighten up and lift up your heads, because your redemption is drawing near. Then He told them a parable: Behold the fig tree and all the trees; as soon as they put forth leaves, you see it and know for yourselves that summer is now near. So you also, when you see these things happening, recognize that the kingdom of God is near. Truly I say to you, **this generation will not pass away until all things take place**. (Luke 21:27–32; emphasis added)

Yeshua is explicitly stating that the people he is talking to will see the things he is talking about take place. The first verse makes this fact completely unavoidable... "**there are some of those who are standing here who will not taste death until they see the Son of Man coming in His kingdom**." This "coming in his kingdom" is with the "glory of his Father and his angels" and will accompany the payment of "every man according to his deeds." In other words, Yeshua's triumphant return and the judgment day. This isn't some "secret," "hidden" or "spiritual" event. This was something that was going to happen sometime during the generation (i.e., lifetime) of those that were listening to him.

> But Jesus kept silent and the high priest said to Him, "I adjure you by the living God, that you tell us whether you are the Christ, the Son of God." Jesus said to him, "You have said it yourself; nevertheless, I tell you, hereafter **you will see the Son of Man sitting at the right hand of power, and coming on the clouds of heaven**." (Matthew 26:63, 64; emphasis added)

Here Yeshua is explicitly telling the high priest that he personally would see him "**coming on the clouds of heaven**." Now let's look at what the New Testament authors believed.

> Long ago, at many times and in many ways, God spoke to our fathers by the prophets, but **in these last days** he has spoken to us by his Son… (Hebrews 1:1–2; emphasis added)

> Now these things happened to them as an example, but they were written down for our instruction, on whom **the end of the ages has come**. (1 Corinthians 10:11; emphasis added)

> And let us consider how to stir up one another to love and good works, not neglecting to meet together, as is the habit of some, but encouraging one another,

and all the more as **you see the Day drawing near**. (Hebrews 10:24–25; emphasis added)

Children, **it is the last hour**, and as you have heard that antichrist is coming, so now many antichrists have come. Therefore we know that **it is the last hour**. (1 John 2:18; emphasis added)

Do not seek a wife. This is what I mean, brothers: the appointed time has grown very short. From now on, let those who have wives live as though they had none, and those who mourn as though they were not mourning, and those who rejoice as though they were not rejoicing, and those who buy as though they had no goods, and those who deal with the world as though they had no dealings with it. For **the present form of this world is passing away**. (1 Corinthians 7:27,29–31; emphasis added)

The end of all things is near…(1 Peter 4:7; emphasis added)

The people that wrote these words clearly believed the end of the world was near and Yeshua was going to return at any moment.

For this we declare to you by a word from the Lord, that **we who are alive, who are left until the coming of the Lord**, will not precede those who have fallen asleep. For the Lord himself will descend from heaven with a cry of command, with the voice of an archangel, and with the sound of the trumpet of God. And the dead in Christ will rise first. Then **we who are alive, who are left, will be caught up together with them in the clouds to meet the Lord in the air**, and so we will always be with the Lord. (1 Thessalonians 4:15–17; emphasis added)

We shall not all sleep, but we shall all be changed. (1 Cor. 15:51)

...**the coming of the Lord is near**...**the Judge is standing right at the door**. (James 5:8, 9)

Here the authors are telling the people they are writing to that Yeshua was coming in their day. They also recognize that some believers were already getting concerned about the lack of fulfillment of Yeshua's prediction since some of the believers had already died. Note the consistent use of the word "we." Obviously they aren't talking about Christians a couple of millennia in the future. They are talking about themselves and the other believers alive at that time.

Blessed is he who reads and those who hear the words of the prophecy, and heed the things which are written in it; for **the time is near**. (Revelation 1:3; emphasis added)

And he said to me, "These words are faithful and true"; and the Lord, the God of the spirits of the prophets, sent His angel to show to His bond-servants the things which **must soon take place**. "And behold, **I am coming quickly**. Blessed is he who heeds the words of the prophecy of this book." And he said to me, "Do not seal up the words of the prophecy of this book, for **the time is near**. Behold, **I am coming quickly**, and My reward is with Me, to render to every man according to what he has done. He who testifies to these things says, '**Yes, I am coming quickly.**'" (Revelation 22:6, 7, 10, 12, 20; emphasis added)

After Yeshua's proclamation that some of those listening to him would still be alive when he returned, there is no way that whoever was talking to John in the Revelation could repeatedly say "soon," "time is near," and "I am coming quickly" if what he really meant was—you know, some time in the next two thousand years or so.

That would be intentionally and horribly misleading to the people the book was written to. Let's look at a number of the excuses that the apologists have come up with over the last two thousand years to try to spin and obfuscate that simple fact.

1. **In Matthew 16:28, Yeshua was referring to his transfiguration instead of his second coming.**

The transfiguration is recorded in Matthew 17, Mark 9, and Luke 9. But Mark and Luke place the time of the transfiguration at a different time than Matthew. In Matthew, it happens after Yeshua states that some of the people listening to him would not die before they saw him coming in his kingdom. Apologists try to claim that the transfiguration was in fact Yeshua "coming in his kingdom." To call that stretching would be a gross understatement at best. There was no "coming with the angels" and no "reward for every man according to his deeds"—which pretty much blows that theory out of the water. And just to double tap the dead theory, in both Mark and Luke the transfiguration happens **before** Yeshua's prediction, not after.

2. **The word translated "generation" can also mean "race." So Yeshua meant the Jewish race would still exist when he returned.**

Grasping at straws is the thought that comes to mind with this one. I don't believe there is anywhere in the Bible where it even remotely implies that the Jews might possibly be completely exterminated. That would kind of defeat the whole purpose, wouldn't it? The word "generation" in the New Testament means the people living at a particular point in time, not some race of people.

3. **"This generation shall not pass away" means the generation living through the tribulation at the end of time.**

Yeshua's followers in the first century were certainly living in tribulation. Being slaughtered for your beliefs is about as tribulating as it gets. It's very apparent from the writers of the New Testament that they believed they were living in the fulfillment of Yeshua's description of the trials and troubles of the end times. Also, if Yeshua wasn't referring to the people of his time, he would have said "that generation," not "this generation."

4. **Yeshua was talking about the day of Pentecost.**

Um, no. He didn't return on the day of Pentecost. And again, there was no "coming with the angels" no "reward for every man according to his deeds" nor any of the other things that are supposed to happen at his return that occurred on the day of Pentecost.

5. **Time scales in John's vision (Revelation) have to be understood from God's perspective. To God, *a thousand years are like a day* (see Psalm 90:4 and 2 Peter 3:8).**

First, I would point out that any God or angel would be perfectly aware of what humans will think when you use terms like "soon," "time is near," and "I am coming quickly." To use terms like that and then argue that they were used relative to a time frame that no human would associate with those words would imply the God or an angel was purposely being deceptive.

This excuse was actually first used by the writer of 2 Peter. It's a clear indication that even the believers in that time were having a hard time understanding how the gospel could be true when it had been so long since Yeshua's ascension and yet he still hadn't returned as promised. 2 Peter 3:4 also provides a pretty good clue that 2 Peter wasn't written by Peter the disciple. *"Where is the promise of His coming? For since the fathers fell asleep, all things continue as they were from the beginning of creation."* The part about the *"fathers fell asleep"* is a reference to the original "fathers" of the church, which would most likely include the disciple Peter. In verse 8, the writer states, *"With the Lord, a day is like a thousand years, and a thousand years are like a day"* and then continues in verse 9 to argue that the Lord is not being slow in his return, he just wants to make sure everyone has a chance to be saved.

Whether it was written by the original disciple or not, it's clearly an attempt to reassure some doubting believers that Yeshua was indeed still going to be coming soon. Over 1,900 years, later they're still saying the same thing: soon.

6. **Yeshua was referring to his ascension as "coming in his kingdom."**

This one fails for the same reasons that the Day of Pentecost excuse fails. Once again, none of the things that are supposed to happen at his return occurred at the ascension. There was no "coming with the angels" no "reward for every man according to his deeds," etc.

Speaking of which, Yeshua's ascension is recorded in Mark, Luke, and Acts. I find it quite odd that something as important as Yeshua's ascension wouldn't be mentioned in Matthew or John. Most biblical scholars agree that the verses in Mark (16:9–19) describing the ascension **were added later**. Those verses are not in the oldest copies of Mark. This is even noted in the NIV version of the Bible. In *A Textual Commentary on the Greek New Testament*, Bruce Metzger wrote, "Clement of Alexandria and Origen [early third century] show no knowledge of the existence of these verses. Furthermore, Eusebius and Jerome attest that the passage was absent from almost all Greek copies of Mark known to them." The language and style of the Greek in these verses is clearly not the same as the rest of Mark.

Most biblical scholars also agree that Luke and Acts were written by the same (unknown) author and that they were originally two parts of the same book. Interestingly, in Luke it seems that Yeshua's ascension occurred on the same day as his resurrection. But in Acts, his ascension occurred forty days after the resurrection. A rather big discrepancy if both books were written by the same person. Actually, a really big discrepancy, period.

7. **Yeshua couldn't have meant he was going to return in the first century because that didn't happen, and if that's what he meant, then it would prove he was a false prophet.**

Of the seven excuses, this one is the most enlightening. It's a perfect example of the power of belief to completely override all logic and reason. Let me explain the thread of illogic someone must use to believe this "explanation." Since Yeshua couldn't be wrong (he was the son of God, the Messiah, the redeemer), and since the Bible can't be wrong (it's God's inerrant Word), therefore Yeshua simply couldn't have meant what he clearly said because that isn't what happened. They *admit* that what he said isn't what happened. They *admit* that if that was what he meant, then he would have to be a false prophet. But then they just argue that what he clearly said isn't what he actually meant.

Let's look at this another way. Assume that it was written in the Koran, that Muhammad had promised people listening to him that some of them would still be alive when he returned after his death. Every Christian would know that verse, and it would be used as **absolute proof** that Muhammad was a fraud because **IT DIDN'T HAPPEN**. Not a single Christian would argue, or accept the argument, that Muhammad didn't actually mean what he very clearly said. Yet that's exactly what they're trying to get you to believe when applied to Yeshua.

For Christian believers, it's virtually impossible to accept that what Yeshua said in those verses is what he actually meant. If they did, they would have to accept that what they believe is wrong, so their belief simply overpowers their reason. If Yeshua's prediction that "**some of those who are standing here who will not taste death until they see the Son of Man coming in His kingdom**" didn't happen, then Yeshua *is* a false prophet according to the Bible. "*You may say to yourself, How can we recognize a message the Lord has not spoken? When a prophet speaks in the Lord's name, and the message does not* *come true or is not fulfilled, that is a message the Lord has not spoken. The prophet has spoken it presumptuously. Do not be afraid of him"* (Deuteronomy 18:21–22).

If a prophet, messenger of God, angel, or Messiah makes a prediction that doesn't come true, well, that means he's not really talking to, or for, God. You don't have to worry about anything he says. Ellen G. White, the "prophetess" that was one of the founders of the Seventh Day Adventist church, also told a number of people that some of them would not die before Yeshua returned. They're all dead. She died in 1915.

> If a prophet or someone who has dreams arises among you and proclaims a sign or wonder to you, and that sign or wonder he has promised you comes about, but he says, "Let us follow other gods," which you have not known, "and let us worship them," do not listen to that prophet's words or to that dreamer. For the Lord your God is testing you to know whether you love the Lord your God with all your heart and all your soul. You must follow the Lord your God and fear him. **You must keep his commands and listen to him; you must worship him and remain faithful to him. That prophet or dreamer must be put to death**, because he has urged rebellion against the Lord your God who brought you out of the land of Egypt and redeemed you from the place of slavery,

to turn you from the way the Lord your God has commanded you to walk. You must purge the evil from you. (Deuteronomy 13:1–5; emphasis added)

Hmmm… It's interesting to consider those verses in the context of a new prophet or "messiah" working all sorts of "signs and wonders" while at the same time claiming to be the "son of God" and the new heir to the throne. And then that "messiah's" followers claiming that he is in fact the God of old just "incarnated" into a human form and that he is to be worshipped as their "savior"—well, it kinda makes you wonder.

As I pointed out in the previous chapter, Judaism and Christianity are two different religions with two different Gods based on two different books: the Old and New Testaments. It's undeniable that Yeshua and his disciples started a new religion. If they didn't, Christianity wouldn't exist today. It's also undeniable that Yeshua is the god of Christianity. The book of John repeatedly states that Yeshua was at least ***a*** god if not ***the*** god.

> In the beginning was the Word, and the Word was with God, and the Word was God. (John 1:1)

> And the Word was made flesh, and dwelt among us (and we beheld his glory, the glory as of the only begotten of the Father) full of grace and truth. (John 1:14)

> For the law was given by Moses, but grace and truth came by Jesus Christ. No man hath seen God at any time, the only begotten Son, which is in the bosom of the Father, he hath declared him. (John 1:17–18)

From reading the book of John, it is obvious that the "Word" the author is talking about is Yeshua. Consequently, it's quite clear that John was in fact teaching the people to follow and worship a new god: Yeshua. Recognizing this problem, the Catholic Church **made up** the concept of the "Holy Trinity." While the New Testament repeatedly mentions the Father, Son, and Holy Ghost, nowhere does it ever say or even imply that they are actually the same person. The Trinity concept is just an attempt to make Yeshua god while trying to avoid the fact that they are replacing Yahweh with Yeshua. It's just one of many falsehoods that the Catholics have made up that have become part of Christian dogma.

Another interesting point in John 1:18 is the claim that *"No man hath seen God at any time."* Like many other statements in the New Testament, it almost seems like the authors weren't aware of, or else simply ignored, facts clearly stated in the Old Testament. In Genesis, God apparently often walked in the garden *"in the cool of the day"* (Genesis 2:8). Adam and Eve were obviously aware of this (meaning they were used to **seeing** Him) and hid from Him (so He wouldn't **see** them) after eating the forbidden fruit. But He calls them out and then proceeds to question and condemn them for committing their great sin. It strongly indicates they were talking face to face; i.e., Adam and Eve **saw** Him. In Exodus 33, Moses asked to see God. While God would not allow him to see His face, Moses did get to see His back. Even better, in Exodus 18, Abraham actually had lunch with God—face to face. When the writer of John claims that *"**no man** has seen God at **any time**,"* based on what anyone can read in the Bible, he's obviously quite wrong.

Let's look at some other New Testament problems: the genealogy of Joseph (the husband of Mary, the mother of Yeshua) and Yeshua. Matthew and Luke both give the genealogy of Joseph (Matthew 1:2–17 and Luke 3:23–38). Unfortunately, like many other stories in the New Testament, they don't agree with each other. In fact, they don't even agree on who Joseph's father was. Remember, this is supposedly the inerrant word of God. The apologists try to claim that the genealogy in Luke is actually Mary's genealogy. But, unfortunately, Luke explicitly states that it is Joseph's genealogy (Luke 3:23).

The purpose of both versions of Joseph's genealogy is to show that he (and consequently Yeshua) was a direct descendant of King David. The first question to ask here is, what difference does it make who Joseph was descended from since, supposedly, he wasn't the father of Yeshua anyway? Supposedly, according to the New Testament, God was Yeshua's father. If that's the case, then Joseph's genealogy is totally irrelevant.

It's also interesting to note that **only** Matthew and Luke list Joseph's genealogy and **only** Matthew and Luke mention the virgin birth. This is the first clue that the "virgin birth" story was added to the original writings of Matthew and Luke. Matthew lists four women in the genealogy: Tamar, who pretended to be a whore to become pregnant by her father-in-law (Genesis 38:12–19); Rahab, who was a whore that lived in the city of Jericho (Joshua 2:1); Ruth, who slipped into bed with Boaz who later married her (Ruth 3:1–14); and Bathsheba, the adulteress that was impregnated by King David (2 Samuel 11:2–5). Two whores, one adulteress, and one of questionable morality. An interesting list of women, to say the least. Might it be a way of softening or excusing Mary's pre-marriage pregnancy before the story of the virgin birth was added?

As I pointed out earlier, Matthew (1:22–23) tries to claim that the virgin birth was the fulfillment of a prophecy in Isaiah Chapter 7 regarding the virgin birth of a son that was to be named Immanuel. As I also pointed out earlier, the prophecy in Isaiah has nothing to do with Yeshua and, if it did, he should have been named Immanuel, not Yeshua.

Matthew also claims that Mary, Joseph, and Yeshua's return from Egypt was a fulfillment of a prophecy in Hosea 11:1. But, like many preachers do today, Matthew only quotes the second half of the verse (the practice of "cherry picking"). When read in context, it is blatantly apparent that the verse is referring to when Moses led the people of Israel out of Egypt. The very next verse (Hosea 11:2 NIV) states, *"But the more they were called, the more they went away from me. They sacrificed to the Baals and they burned incense to images."* Does that sound like it's referring to the Messiah?

Matthew, Mark, Luke, and John all record Yeshua's "triumphant" entry into Jerusalem, riding on a donkey. But in Matthew, there are **two** animals, a donkey and a colt, mentioned repeatedly, and Yeshua was riding on both of them (Matthew 21:1–7). This isn't a mistake that can be blamed on different perspectives of the witnesses. While the disciples may have been mostly simple fishermen, even a fisherman wouldn't mistake a single donkey for multiple animals.

Why Matthew has two animals becomes clear when you realize that when the author of Matthew was scouring through the Old Testament for anything that could possibly be interpreted as a prophecy of a Messiah, he misunderstood Zechariah 9:9, which states that the king would be *"riding upon an ass* ***and*** *upon a colt, the foal of an ass."* If the author had looked at, or understood, the Old Testament Hebrew, he would have known that the word translated as "and" was not referring to another animal but is actually used as "even," for emphasis. In addition, when read in context, it's quite obvious the conditions Zechariah is describing in Chapter 9 are not the conditions of Yeshua's time.

What Matthew's mistaken story of two animals clearly illustrates is that the "triumphant entry" story is not based on an actual event, or at least not on an accurate telling of the event (if it was, it would agree with Mark, Luke, and John about a single donkey) but is instead a story attempting to create a "fulfillment" of a "prophecy" about a Messiah in spite of the fact that the original Old Testament text wasn't referring to any Messiah. Another thing it clearly illustrates is that, like most of the New Testament authors, whoever wrote Matthew was not a scholar of the Old Testament. It's also apparent the author wasn't reading the Hebrew version of the Old Testament and may not have known Hebrew at all. Finally, it's more proof that the author was definitely not Matthew the disciple or any other eyewitness to a "triumphant entry."

In Matthew 27:3–9, there is the story of Judas taking the thirty pieces of silver back to the priests and then throwing them down in the temple. The priests then took the thirty pieces of silver and bought a potter's field to bury strangers in. In verse 9, Matthew claims this was to fulfill what the prophet **Jeremiah** said, and then he quotes **Zechariah** 11:12–13 (***not Jeremiah***) as the prophecy that was fulfilled. Read Zechariah 11. You'll find Zechariah is describing actions that he did as God directed. While it can be argued that Zechariah is acting out some metaphorical charade of a message God is sending to the people, there is nothing in the story referring to a Messiah or a betrayal or anything else resembling the events that Matthew claims Judas's betrayal and interaction with the priests fulfilled.

Again, what we are seeing is very sloppy attempts to find anything in the Old Testament that can be taken out of context and twisted into some sort of messianic prophecy that the author can then claim events of Yeshua's story fulfilled. In this case, he can't even get the name of the prophet he is quoting correct. Remember, this is supposedly the inerrant, inspired word of God.

Only Matthew (27:51–53) tells the story of graves being opened and many saints being raised from the dead during the earthquake that occurred when Yeshua died. He says that the resurrected saints went into the city and were seen by many. You would think someone besides Matthew might have mentioned something as miraculous as a bunch of dead people being resurrected and visiting people in Jerusalem, but apparently he's the only one that thought it was significant enough to mention. None of the other gospels mention it. Hmm...

Matthew 28:1 and Mark 16:1 state that Mary Magdalene and Mary the mother of James found the tomb of Yeshua empty on Sunday morning after the crucifixion. Luke 23:55–24:1 adds Joanna, and mentions other unnamed women that were with the two Marys. John 20:1–4 states that Mary Magdalene went to the tomb alone then went and got Peter and another disciple and took them to the tomb.

All four gospels have differing versions of an angel, angels, and a young man the various people that went to the tomb found there. Matthew 28:9 says the women ran into Yeshua after leaving the tomb. John 20:14 says Mary Magdalene saw Yeshua at the tomb.

Luke 24:51 is the only gospel that describes Yeshua's ascension into heaven. I find it hard to believe that something as miraculous as seeing a person float up off the ground and ascend into the sky wouldn't be included in every account of anyone that witnessed the event and was documenting the life story of the person that ascended into the sky, while Mark 16:19 makes mention that after talking to them (the disciples), Yeshua *"was received up into heaven and sat on the right hand of God."* Most biblical scholars agree that verses 9–20 were added to the Gospel of Mark by an unknown author after it was originally written. Acts 1:9–12 also describes the ascension and then includes a story of two "men in white apparel" suddenly appearing and talking to the disciples as they were staring up into the sky where Yeshua had gone.

In Luke, the ascension happens in Bethany on the same day as the resurrection. In Acts, it happens on Mount Olivet forty days after the resurrection. It's interesting that most biblical scholars think Luke and Acts are simply two parts of the same original book. How sloppy of an author would you have to be to tell the same story twice in one book with completely contradictory details?

The examples listed above are merely a sample of the many contradictions and inaccuracies of the New Testament. While the Christian churches and apologists have made up a never-ending list of excuses and "explanations" trying to reconcile the contradictions, none of them can pass the "smell" test, much less the simple logic test. Most are blatantly absurd, while many more are so convoluted that the apparent goal is simply to baffle you until you've completely forgotten what the original question was. Having done even a minimal study of these contradictions, there is no way anyone can honestly claim that the New Testament is, in any sense, the infallible, inerrant Word of God.

There are over four different Christian philosophies of how eternal life is obtained, categorized as Selection, Predestination, Justification by Faith, Justification by Works, etc.—all of which can legitimately be demonstrated, supported, and "proven" by the New Testament. And they all contradict each other!

The simple fact is that what we are told that Yeshua and his followers believed is just wrong. But as clear as that is to an unbiased person, to the Christian, it just can't be true. If Yeshua wasn't the son of God and the Messiah, then the New Testament is just a sad story and there is no basis for Christianity. Without Christianity, there is no basis for the Catholic or any other Christian denomination. Like a house of cards, the whole religion of Christianity falls apart.

Although I could be wrong, I tend to believe there was a man named Yeshua who became a bit of a revolutionary leader, exposing the hypocrisy and failings of the religious leaders of his time. He may have believed that he was a son of God, a reformer, a Messiah. And he may have convinced a number of other people to believe that. Unfortunately, like many other Messiahs throughout history that dared to stand up and speak out against the leaders of their time, he wound up getting himself killed. But that made him a martyr and a hero. And like many other dead martyrs and heroes, they become the stuff of legends, and the stories keep getting bigger and better until they are finally deified and hailed as Gods. Making Gods of dead, and even living, kings and heroes was quite in fashion in the days of Rome, when all of the New Testament stories were written.

Unfortunately, when you learn and honestly, objectively consider all of the facts regarding the authorship, the discrepancies between the stories, the multiple versions and obvious modifications of the writings, the discrepancies between church dogma and the actual writings, and the foretold events that simply didn't happen, the only honest conclusion you can come to is that the New Testament is not even remotely close to being the authoritative, inerrant word of God upon which to base your beliefs. For the Christian churches, as bad as it is, it's the only basis they have to justify their existence and get people to donate their time and money.

I could write another ten chapters on various issues with the New Testament, but it would be a waste of my time. Many other authors have already documented and analyzed those issues in great detail. The sincere seeker of the truth can, and will, find and read those.

CHAPTER 6

GOD'S LEADERSHIP

In most religions, questioning anything regarding the religion or its leaders is frowned upon. Questioning the Supreme Being is not just frowned upon but often considered downright blasphemous. Why is that? Do you really think that a being capable of creating the entire universe and every living thing in it would get upset, annoyed, or even angry because something equivalent to an ant, compared to Himself, would question, judge, or criticize Him? Would **you** care if an ant questioned, judged, or criticized you? Of course not.

Does any normal rational parent get violently upset and angry when their four-year-old throws a temper tantrum and screams "I hate you" because the parent wouldn't let them have another ice cream cone? While they might give them a little swat on the hiney to encourage them to behave, they certainly aren't going to beat them and condemn them to life in prison over it. Yet, most Christians seem to think that the kind, loving God they believe in will allow all sorts of evil to afflict them and condemn them to everlasting hell if they dare to question Him. Do you really think that the God of the universe is so insecure that He needs your absolute, unquestioning, unthinking submission? Did He really give you a brain and then expect you not to use it? I don't think so. Only tyrants act that way.

While I no longer believe in the God of Christianity, I wrote this chapter for the sake of discussion from the perspective of, OK let's assume the view of God as taught in Christian religions today is actually true. He is the Yahweh of the Old Testament and the kind, loving, heavenly Father of the New Testament. He is the creator and master of the universe. Everything from the laws of physics to the colorations of the iris of an eye were made by Him. He gave Moses the Ten Commandments and agreed on the rest of the Mosaic laws that, at least, the Israelites were supposed to live by. So let's take a minute to consider the history of the Christian God as presented in the Bible.

But before we do, I should warn you that if you're not comfortable with an honest, critical, and, quite frankly, often unflattering analysis of God's interaction and leadership, you might want to skip this chapter. Personally, I don't believe in the concept that something is so sacred that it must not be questioned or honestly evaluated. I don't believe the truth has any fear of questions or is offended by honest evaluation. But that's me. If you feel different, then, as I said, feel free to skip this chapter.

Among Christians, it is generally agreed that the angels were created during or perhaps before the six days of creation in Genesis. According to Job 38:4–7, the angels were present when the earth's foundation was laid. In any case, for our purposes, they existed before humans were made. So we have these perfect beings living in a perfect heaven. And then what happened? There was war in heaven where one-third of the angels rebelled. Exactly when this war took place is also a matter of debate, but again, for our purposes, it doesn't really matter when it happened. The point is that one-third of the angels rebelled and were kicked out of heaven (their home).

The next beings created according to the story are the humans. God made two of them, Adam and Eve. And then what happened? Before they could even begin to fulfill the command to *"be fruitful and multiply"* (Genesis 1:28), they rebelled (sinned) and ate the forbidden fruit. So they were kicked out of the Garden (their home).

The next two humans in the story are Cain and Abel. We all know what happened here. Even after God had a talk with Cain about his anger (Genesis 4:6–7), he ignored that and killed his brother Abel. And what was his punishment? Pay attention, there are two important points here.

1. From the God that required a life for a life (Genesis 9:5–6, Deuteronomy 19:2), the God that never changes, His punishment of Cain was rather odd. Cain knew what he deserved and was afraid that anyone that found him would kill him (Genesis 4:14). But instead, God protected him (a murderer) by putting some sort of mark on him. As you read the Bible, pay attention to how God treats murderers.

2. God's "punishment" was to make him a *"fugitive and a vagabond"* (Genesis 4:12); i.e., kicked out of his home. Notice the beginning of a pattern? Getting kicked out of home.

It seems that for many centuries humans were more or less free to live as they saw fit until God decided they had all become evil. So he drowned them all with a flood—everyone except Noah and his family. For a number of centuries after the flood, it again seems like humans more or less did what they wanted, although God did interfere at the Tower of Babel and divided the people by giving them different languages. But starting with Abraham, God personally took charge of a group of people that came to be known as the Israelites, Hebrews, or Jews. God changed the name of Abraham's grandson Jacob to Israel. Israel had twelve sons. The descendants of those sons became the twelve tribes of Israel. They are Yahweh's special chosen people, and He is their personal God.

Around 215 years after Abraham arrived in Canaan, his descendants went to Egypt to escape a famine. After around 210 years of living in Egypt, God chooses Moses (a murderer) to take His people out of Egypt and settle them in "the Promised Land" of Canaan. On a side note, many Christians will point out that the Bible clearly states that the Israelites were in Egypt for 400 years (two verses: Genesis 15:13 and Acts 7:6) or 430 years (two verses: Exodus 12:41, Galatians 3:17). But the Bible also gives ages and timelines (Genesis 21:5, 25:26, 47:9, and others) that make it clear that the Israelites weren't actually in Egypt for 400 or 430 years. But don't take my word for it, research it yourself. Anyway, back to the history.

The first time the people of Israel reached the border of the Promised Land (Canaan), they were afraid of the inhabitants and refused to invade on the day God told them to. The very next day they repented (said they were sorry) and were willing to invade. But it was too late. God was angry and condemned them to wander around outside of Canaan until everyone that was over the age of twenty at the time had died (except Joshua and Caleb). This time they weren't kicked out of their home, they simply weren't allowed in (see Numbers 14:1–35).

From the time of Moses until the anointing of Saul as the first king of Israel, the highest level of authority were the "judges" and the priests. During that time, the Israelites were often under the control of various enemy tribes, such as the Moabites, Philistines, Midianites, etc. Like many time periods in the Bible, it's not exactly clear, or agreed upon, how long the period of the judges lasted—somewhere between 350 to 450 years. For our purposes, it doesn't matter how long it was. What matters is **why** it ended. The last judge was Samuel, who was also a priest. It was during his time as judge that the Israelite people demanded a king to rule over them.

Samuel was raised in the temple by the high priest Eli. Eli's two sons were bad men that abused their position as priests. Unfortunately, although Eli warned his sons, he wouldn't actually discipline them or remove them from the priesthood. Finally, God had had enough and told Eli all of his descendants were cursed and that as a sign of this curse, his two sons would die on the same day (1 Samuel 2:12–34 and 1 Samuel 3:11–14). Some time later, in a big battle with their Philistine enemies, both of Eli's sons were killed and the sacred ark of the covenant was captured (1 Samuel 4:10). The same day, a messenger told Eli about it, and he fell off his chair, broke his neck, and died (1 Samuel 4:18).

The purpose of recounting the story of Eli and his sons is because Samuel also had two sons. When Samuel got older, he appointed his two sons as judges. But, just like Eli's sons, Samuel's sons were bad guys that lined their pockets, took bribes, and perverted justice (1 Samuel 8:1–3). After a few centuries of living in a theocratic form of government, the Israelite people were fed up with being ruled by corrupt priests and judges, so they demanded that Samuel appoint a king. Most Christian commentaries like to focus on the part of the elder's statement that they wanted a king *"as all the other nations have"* and then they like to gloss over the first reason given; i.e., because Samuel was old and **his sons (the judges) were corrupt** (1 Samuel 8:5).

Nobody likes living under corrupt rulers. In a theocracy, the leaders are the representatives of God. As you read the history of the Israelites in the Bible, it's amazing how often the rulers, God's representatives (priests, judges, kings, and prophets), are absolutely evil people. Although there are a few exceptions, it's even more amazing how rarely the almighty God punished or did anything about those evil rulers. What kind of leadership is that?

Anyway, we now get to the point where Samuel appoints the first king of Israel. It's important to note that God Himself chose Saul to be the first king of Israel (1 Samuel 9:15–17). It's also interesting to note that Saul was *"as handsome a young man as could be found anywhere in Israel, and he was a head taller than anyone else"* (1 Samuel 9:2). So Samuel anointed Saul (1 Samuel 10:1), then gave him a series of instructions about where to go and who he would meet and what he was to do when he met them, culminating with meeting a procession of prophets that would be prophesying. When he met them, the *"Spirit of the Lord will come powerfully upon you, and you will prophesy with them; and you will be changed into a different person"* (1 Samuel 10:6). So, God chose him, Samuel anointed him, and the Spirit of the Lord changed him.

But then, because Saul had not exactly followed God's instructions, God regretted that He had made Saul king and rejected Saul. This is especially odd when you consider that "the Spirit" **changed** Saul into a "different" person. I would assume that the Spirit would make Saul an even more righteous person. But apparently that's not what happened. The important thing to realize here is that this is the God that supposedly knows **everything**, from the beginning to the end. So why would he choose Saul if He was just going to wind up regretting it?

I should point out that the same problem and question applies as to why God made humans at all. Or angels for that matter. According to Genesis 6:5–6, *"When the Lord saw how great the wickedness of human beings was on earth, and how every desire that their heart conceived was always nothing but evil, the Lord regretted making human beings on the earth, and his heart was grieved."* How grievous could it be if God already knew it was going to happen? Or, knowing that He was going to drown them all, why would He make them in the first place? Likewise, why would you not do anything until one-third of the angels rebelled? The honest answer here is that these stories, along with a lot of other texts, make it quite clear that, regardless of what the preachers like to claim, God doesn't actually know the future.

OK, back to our review of God's leadership. Having rejected Saul, God chooses David to be the next king of Israel (1 Samuel 16:1). Again, note that God is the one choosing the king. The Bible claims that David was a "man after God's own heart" (1 Samuel 13:14), a man that God apparently considered to be much like Himself, which is interesting when you consider David's faults, including adultery and murder. Once again, it seems God has a soft spot for murderers.

It's also interesting to read the punishments God inflicted when David messed up. Invariably it's someone else that pays the price. The child born as a result of David's adultery dies a few days after birth. David's sons Amnon and Absalom both wind up dead because David wouldn't discipline Amnon for raping his sister Tamar. Before being killed, Absalom leads a rebellion and briefly takes over the kingdom and the palace.

While he is in the palace, Absalom has sex with David's ten "favorite" concubines, who David purposely left there. When David retakes the palace, he condemns those ten "favorite" concubines to live the rest of their lives in prison. Think about that. He purposely left them there and then condemns them to die in prison for something they had no choice in. A man after God's own heart.

God kills seventy thousand **other** people because David counted all of his fighting men, people that had absolutely nothing to do with David's choice. While preachers like to point out that David always felt bad and repented for his mistakes, I seriously doubt that would provide much comfort to the seventy thousand that died or their loved ones.

The question is, why doesn't God punish the person that actually annoyed Him? In the Law that God gave Moses, the punishment for both adultery and murder was execution. But just like today, whether the prescribed punishment according to the law is actually applied apparently depends on who you are. The preachers like to use that as an example of how merciful and forgiving God is. To me, it's an example of hypocrisy. "Do as I say, not as I do." And again, tell all those that died and lost friends and family as a result of God punishing David that it's because of God's mercy and forgiveness.

On a sidenote, there are a couple of other things to point out regarding God's leadership. You can't find anywhere in the Bible where God had a problem with either slavery or polygamy (having multiple wives). Many of God's special people had multiple wives. In fact, the twelve sons of Jacob (Israel), and consequently the twelve tribes of Israel came from one father and four different mothers (two wives, two concubines). Abraham had two sons from two different women (one wife, one concubine). David had at least seven wives that are named in the Bible and more that aren't named. Solomon had seven hundred wives and three hundred concubines, and he was the one that God chose to build the temple. The point is, if God had a problem with polygamy or slavery, He would have said something about it, but He didn't. Although we consider both polygamy and slavery evil practices today, God apparently doesn't have a problem with either one. Kinda odd, isn't it?

According to the Bible, one of the worst kings of Israel—if not **the** worst—was Manasseh. *"Manasseh also shed so much innocent blood that he filled Jerusalem with it from one end to another"* (2 Kings 21:16). He was a mass murderer. It's interesting to note that he also reigned **longer than any other king of Israel**. He was captured and imprisoned by the Assyrians but then, after praying to God, he was restored as king of Israel. Since he was the most evil king Israel ever had, why would God have the Assyrians set him free and then restore him as Israel's king? Again, God seems to have a soft spot for murderers.

It turns out that the majority of the kings of Israel were bad men. Just as Eli and Samuel couldn't control their rotten kids, it seems God couldn't control the majority of the Hebrew kings. It seems odd that the Almighty has such bad luck with His creations and His personally chosen people. But it gets worse.

After Solomon's reign from 970 to 931 BC, the kingdom of Israel splits into two separate kingdoms: Israel and Judah. For the next 150 years, if they aren't fighting anyone else, God's special chosen people are fighting each other. Eventually, the ten tribes of Israel were conquered and removed from their homeland by the Assyrians in 722 BC. The remaining tribes, known as Judah, were conquered and taken captive by the Babylonians in 586 BC. Starting around forty-seven years later, with the permission of Cyrus the Great, they began migrating back to their homeland from Babylon.

From there, they lived as a subject state to the Persians until Alexander the Great conquered the Persians, at which point they became part of the Seleucid Empire, one of the empires resulting in the division of Alexander the Great's Macedonian Empire. In 167 BC, the Jews revolted in what is known as the Maccabean Revolt. In 140 BC, they succeeded in expelling the Syrian Greeks and once again became an independent kingdom. That lasted about 80 years until 63 BC when the Romans invaded them. In 37 BC, Herod became the Roman client king of Israel. In 70 AD, the

Romans destroyed Jerusalem and the Second Temple.

Like everything else in archeology, exactly when Abraham lived is unknown and hotly debated. But for our purposes, it's fairly safe to say it was somewhere between 2300–1900 BC. So, from Abraham, the father of the Israelites, until the destruction of the temple in 70 AD, there were around two thousand-plus years of Israelite history. From the Bible and historical evidence, it's clear that the Israelites were subject to various foreign kingdoms for a large part of that time period, perhaps even the majority. Doesn't it seem a bit odd that the tribe of people that the All-Mighty, All-knowing God, creator of the entire universe, chose to be His special people, that He personally guided and ruled over, would so constantly be defeated and subjugated by their enemies?

God's promise to Abraham was that He would give him more descendants than he could count, that He would give his descendants the land of Canaan forever, and that he would be the father of many nations (Genesis 17:2–7). So how did that work out over the roughly two thousand years from Abraham to the destruction of the second temple in 70 AD? When the Israelites finally entered Canaan after leaving Egypt, they did take over much of the land of Canaan, but not all of it. Over the next few hundred years of the period of the Judges, the Israelites fought with the various kingdoms around them, sometimes winning, sometimes being defeated and living as subjects to the foreigners. They weren't exactly the superpower of the region.

Then began the period of the Kings. Under the first two kings, they held their own or gained a little. Under Solomon, the third king, the nation hit its high point. The economy was great, the first temple was built, and the people were prosperous. Unfortunately, after Solomon, the nation split in two, and then things went downhill. Within 150 years, the ten tribes of Israel were conquered by Assyria and moved from their homeland to somewhere further north, between Assyria and one of Assyria's enemies. From there they more or less disappeared from history and became known today as the "ten lost tribes of Israel."

About 140 years later, the remaining three tribes known as Judah were conquered, Solomon's temple was looted and then destroyed, and the people were taken captive by the Babylonians around 586 BC. From there, other than a brief period of roughly eighty years between around 140 to 63 BC, they were subject to foreign powers, culminating in their subjection and ultimate dispersion by the Romans. So, within roughly two thousand years, they went from a single man (Abraham) to at least a semi-power in the region and then downhill to the point of no longer existing as a nation. That's not a success story. It's also not a fulfillment of God's promise that Abraham's descendants would have the land of Canaan "forever." Or a fulfillment of God's promise through the prophet Nathan to David that his kingdom would endure "forever," Israel would no longer be disturbed by their enemies, and all future kings of Israel would be descendants of David "forever" (2 Samuel 7:10–16).

Let's be honest, that's not what happened. Israel was definitely "disturbed" by their enemies, the kingdom was split in two, and ultimately both were destroyed by their enemies and there no longer was a kingship to be occupied by any descendant of David. Those are the historical facts of Yahweh's leadership of Israel. Most people would consider that a disaster and failure of leadership.

Now, I'd like to take a minute and look at a God-forbidden practice that the Israelites apparently kept falling into over and over, and that God kept punishing them for over and over: idolatry—the practice of making wood, stone, or metal idols and worshiping them. Isaiah even mocks the ignorance of idol worshipers (Isaiah 44:9–20). For years, I wondered why the Israelites would do this. Why would they worship and pray to a piece of wood or stone rather than their God Yahweh, who could supposedly actually do something for them?

Then one day, it dawned on me. The only reason they would do this is because **it didn't make any difference whether you prayed to Yahweh or a rock**. No one would pray to a rock while his neighbor prayed to Yahweh if the results were different. If his crops were eaten by locusts or his cattle died of disease while his neighbor's crops were **not** eaten or his neighbor's cattle **did not** get diseased. People do what works. If the people that worshiped Yahweh didn't have the same problems as people that worshiped idols did, nobody would've worshiped an idol.

So again, the only reason people would worship idols versus worshiping Yahweh is because there was no difference in the outcome. In fact, Job complains that the opposite was true (Job 21:6–15). His non-Yahweh-worshiping neighbors' cattle never failed to successfully breed. They grew old while increasing in power. They lived their lives in peace and prosperity while telling God to "leave them alone." They received all the blessings Job wanted but didn't get—the exact opposite of what a believer in God would expect. Ponder that for a while.

Let's look at God's leadership of Israel in a metaphorical context. Imagine a person that is claimed to be the richest and most brilliant football coach ever. And that person creates his own football team. He is the owner, general manager, and head coach. Then over a twenty-year period, his team has, at best, a 50/50 win/loss average. In other words, they are a middle-of-the-pack football team. And for the last seven years (one-third of the total), they never even make it to the playoffs. Could you honestly claim that that person was, without a doubt, the greatest football owner/coach ever? Would you honestly believe that all of those losing seasons were never the fault of the owner/general manager/head coach? That it was always the fault of lousy players and/or the subordinate coaches? After all, who chose the subordinate coaches? Who chose the players? If you're the business owner, or the CEO, or the captain of the ship, or the top general of the army, and the business fails, or the ship sinks, or you lose the war...Do you just get to blame all the lousy underlings for the failure? Over and over again? Is that how leadership works?

Let's continue our review of history. After the Romans destroyed Jerusalem, slaughtered the inhabitants, and then took the survivors captive in 70 AD, things kept getting worse for the Jews (Israelites). Their persecution and dispersion from their homeland, which began with the captivity and relocation by Assyria in 733 BC, continued over the next several centuries.

Meanwhile, sometime around 1 BC, Yeshua is born. Thirty years later, he becomes a rabbi (teacher) and begins recruiting his followers and spreading his beliefs until he is crucified. Then his disciples and followers continue spreading his teachings and begin the process of deifying him; i.e. turning him into a God.

A few years after Yeshua's death, Saul of Tarsus is converted on the road to Damascus, becomes Paul the Apostle, and begins evangelizing and preaching his own version of Christianity. This is where the Christians first begin separating into two camps: the believers in Yeshua and his personally chosen disciples and the believers in Paul's version of Yeshua.

Within a few years, the conflicts between the disciples' teachings and Paul's teachings led to a meeting in Jerusalem between Paul and Yeshua's disciples (Acts 15:1–19). The two sides agreed that Paul would continue to focus on converting Gentiles and that the Gentiles didn't have to adopt certain Mosaic laws such as circumcision. While it would seem that the two sides came to an agreement at that meeting, the truth is the two sides continued to diverge.

I would highly recommend doing some research on the Ebionites and the Nazarenes. They are two sects of early Christians who, although they believed Yeshua was the last true prophet, did not believe he was the son of God. They considered themselves Christian Jews, believed in Yeshua, and maintained an adherence to the Law of Moses. The Ebionites in particular considered Paul to be a false apostle. I believe these two groups are probably the closest representations of what Yeshua and his disciples actually taught and the true original followers of Yeshua. Yeshua himself was referred to as "the Nazarene." There is not much original information about these groups because they were labeled heretics by the Catholic Church, which did its best to exterminate them. On the other side, because they were followers of Yeshua, they were also despised and killed whenever possible by the Jewish religious leaders of the time.

The two groups of Christians continued to diverge as Paul's followers dropped more and more of the traditional Jewish customs and beliefs while at the same time creating new traditions, such as Sunday worship and deifying Yeshua as the son of God. In 135 AD the church in Jerusalem was destroyed and the few surviving Jewish Christians were scattered when the Jews were expelled from Jerusalem after another revolt against the Romans. This greatly weakened the original Jewish Christian groups.

At about the same time, Marcion of Sinope, a follower of Paul (who he believed to be the only true apostle), was preaching that the God of Yeshua was greater than Yahweh and that Christianity was superior and opposed to Judaism. The idea of two Gods, two religions, and two books that I presented earlier isn't new. Marcion was preaching the same thing in 140 AD. Marcion also published the first known collection of New Testament books, which contained ten books written by Paul and a shorter version of Luke, which was originally simply called "The Gospel." Today it is called the "Gospel of Marcion." While church leaders have claimed for almost two thousand years that Marcion created the "Gospel of Marcion" by removing portions of the Gospel of Luke, many Biblical scholars now believe that the "Gospel of Marcion" is actually the original and the Gospel of Luke is, in fact, the modified version. Do some research on this.

From 70 AD, the growth of Paul's version of Christianity continued throughout the Roman Empire, finally culminating in the conversion of Emperor Constantine. Constantine outlawed the persecution of Christians with the Edict of Milan in 313 AD, which mandated the toleration of all religions. He also put together and presided over the First Council of Nicaea in 325 AD. This was the beginning of the Catholic church. In 380 AD, Catholic Christianity became the official religion of the

Roman Empire and the first execution of a "heretic" occurred in 385 AD. It didn't take long (five years to be exact) from the time the Catholics gained some power to when they started executing people that disagreed with them.

The Catholic church **claims** to be the religion and church that Yeshua and his disciples started. But the evidence actually points to it evolving from the gentile churches that Paul started. Regardless, for the rest of this chapter, let's assume that the New Testament is in fact God's New Covenant with humanity, that the Heavenly Father of the New Testament is Yahweh, and that Yeshua was in fact the son of God and the Messiah. Let's see how that works out.

The Catholic Church is the richest organization on earth today. It's also the most evil organization that has existed over the last two thousand years, if not ever. When it comes to slaughtering people, it makes Hitler, Stalin, and Mao-tse Tung look like mere amateurs. Let me rephrase that. The Catholic Church has killed **far** more people than Hitler, Stalin, and Mao-tse Tung combined. Most of the people it killed were actually Christians. They just didn't happen to believe the Catholic Church was God's Holy Church or that the Pope was God's personal representative on earth. Again, let me be clear here. When I say the Catholic

Church, I'm referring to the organization and its leadership.

The Catholic Church **caused** the Dark Ages—over 1,200 years of ignorance, misery, poverty, and suffering by millions of people all over Europe. They supported and made deals with Mussolini and Hitler during World War II. They aided and provided political cover in the extermination of six million Jews during World War II. They helped get the Nazis out of Germany when they lost the war. They have been molesting children for centuries, which finally has been exposed in the US over the past couple of decades. Yet I'm not aware of a single priest that has gone to jail for it. Isn't that odd? The number of pages it would take to list all of the atrocities of the Catholic Church over the last two thousand years would constitute a very large book of its own. The point is, they are evil. And we are to believe this is God's church?

For over a millennium, the Catholic Church ruled over the monarchs of Europe. They determined who would be king and removed any king that got out of line. Finally, after one hundred years of warfare, beginning in the 1500s, the power of the Catholic Church over the kings of Europe was weakened. According to the peace treaties signed at the Peace of Westphalia in 1648, each king or prince was free to determine the religion of his own state (they could choose between Catholicism, Lutheranism, and Calvinism), and any Christians that were not members of the official state religion were more or less free to practice their own faith. But it wasn't until Napoleon took the Pope captive in 1798, and then the Italian government's confiscation of the Papal States in 1870, that the Catholic Church's power was truly broken. Unfortunately, it was partially repaired in 1929, when Mussolini signed the Lateran Pacts, restoring the Pope's authority and complete control of the Vatican.

According to Christian theology, God won the war with his archenemy, the Devil, when Yeshua was crucified. Yet the Protestant Christian denominations claim that Christianity was corrupted and fell under the Devil's control when Constantine "converted" and merged Christianity with the government. It seems extremely odd that having just won the war, the All-Mighty, All-Knowing God would lose control of his church within three hundred years and allow the Devil to wage war on all of His true believers, especially His chosen people the Jews, for the next 1,600 years. That just doesn't make any sense.

I find it interesting that some of the early Christians (Ebionites, Nazarenes, and others) recognized that Paul was a false apostle. Without Paul's writings, there wouldn't be any basis for many of Christianity's core beliefs today, such as ignoring the Mosaic laws and the Old Testament holidays. His writings are also most of the basis for Catholic beliefs. Protestant Christian denominations like to believe that they are not like the Catholics, yet they maintain beliefs that are misinterpretations and/or complete fabrications made up by the Catholic Church (Martin Luther pointed out ninety-five of them in his Ninety-Five Theses, which started the Reformation)—beliefs such as the Trinity, Sunday worship, worship of Mother Mary, and Purgatory.

Sunday worship is a direct contradiction of the fourth Commandment, which anyone can verify simply by looking in any non-Catholic Bible (Exodus 20:8–11). You can't verify it in a Catholic Bible because the Catholics changed the Ten Commandments (along with other verses they didn't like). They had to change them; otherwise, Catholic practices would be in direct violation of the commandments. Specifically, they eliminated the second Commandment completely, which forbids making and worshiping idols. That just wouldn't do with their worship of figurines of Mother Mary and others. Then they renumbered commandments 4–9 to 3–8. Then they shortened their third Commandment (originally the fourth) to eliminate any reference to the seventh day (Saturday). Then they divided the tenth Commandment into two separate commandments so they could still wind up with a total of ten.

How could an All-Mighty God allow humans to change and corrupt His New Covenant and His Commandments? Although Yahweh generally didn't do anything about an evil king of Israel, there were a number of times He actually did kill them or have them killed. Yet after winning the war, we're supposed to believe God sat back and did nothing for over 1,200 years while humans corrupted His church, His holy writings, and slaughtered His chosen people and other true followers? Really? Was that the plan?

In God's defense, it must be pointed out that His promises to Abraham and David were conditioned by the people of Israel being perpetually obedient to God. But if we are to believe that God knows the future, then He had to have known at the time He made the promises that they would never be fulfilled. In that case, it's hard to see the difference between a promise and a deception. If God knew they would never happen, then why imply that they could? How's that any different than deceiving Abraham, David, and the rest of the people of Israel? God could promise to make you King of the Universe as long as it was conditioned on something He knew was never going to happen.

But, again, I digress. Beginning with the conquering and exiling of most of the population of the Kingdom of Israel (the Northern ten tribes) by the Assyrians around 750 BC, and then the conquering and taking captive the Kingdom of Judah (the other two or three tribes) along with the destruction of Jerusalem and Solomon's temple by Nebuchadnezzar II in 587 BC, the homeland of the Israelites was almost entirely under the control of foreign kingdoms, except for a few very brief periods. In 64 BC, the Romans took over control of what remained of the Israelite homeland and appointed Jewish-Roman client kings to rule over it. That lasted until 6 AD, when Augustus removed the last Jewish king and made Judea a Roman province. From then until 1948, there was no such thing as a kingdom, nation, or homeland of Israelites.

If we accept the Christian viewpoint that the God of Israel is also the God of Christianity, then that's the history of God's leadership over a roughly four-thousand-year period—a predominantly losing tale of being conquered, subjected, persecuted, corrupted, and destroyed. Not exactly what you might consider a successful resume.

How have the Gods of other nations done? Egypt? China? India? Greece? Roman? Perhaps that's not a fair comparison since each of those nations had multiple Gods supposedly working on their behalf.

But when it comes to the rise and fall of empires, it is clear that ancient Israel was never one of the real power players.

Some Christians might claim that as Rome divided into the nations of Europe and transformed into the Roman Catholic Church, which ruled over those nations until the reformation, that that represented the successful supremacy of the God of Israel. If that were true then, unfortunately, they would also have to accept that the God of Israel was the head of the most evil empire the world has ever known. I don't think that qualifies as "success." Furthermore, the Jews (Israelites) have never considered the God of Christianity (Yeshua) to be the same as their God, Yahweh. Nor have they ever accepted the idea that Christianity is the natural evolution of their religion, Judaism.

Of course, Christians will argue that it's not over yet. They say that "soon" God will destroy the evil ones (two-thirds of the entire population of Earth, according to the Book of Revelation), set up His kingdom, and rule victoriously. As of 2020, the world's population is roughly 7.8 billion people. So, according to Revelation, if God were to commence His final "judgments" today, He would kill 5.14 billion human beings on His way to victory. To put that in perspective, in 1945, the United States had just won World War II, was the sole possessor of nuclear weapons, and the world's population was around 2.25 billion. The US population was about 140 million. If the US had nuked all of Asia, Africa, most of Europe, and most of the Middle East (about two out of every three people on Earth), it would have destroyed all of its potential competition and could have ruled the entire world victoriously, following the Biblical blueprint for success.

I would also point out that according to Revelation, after one thousand years of the direct rule of Yeshua, the entire world rebels (Revelation 20:7–9)—once again following the pattern of every group of beings that the God of the Bible has ruled over. And once again, following the historical pattern, that God kills everyone who isn't willing to bow down and serve him.

If we accept the story of God as presented by Christianity, I find it more than a little odd that every group of beings He rules over ends up rebelling. Why would anyone rebel against a God that is supposedly perfect—omniscient, omnipotent, and pure love? When you compare the Christian claims of what God is against the history of His leadership over angels and humans, it just doesn't add up. This is another reason I don't believe it's true. I don't believe a God that could create our universe and everything in it would repeatedly fail to achieve His goals for a nation or any group of beings, such as angels, that He was in charge of. What would human history look like if we assumed it was all a result of just human leadership? Other than the very beginning of humanity, I think it would look pretty much exactly as we see it.

CHAPTER 7

GENESIS REVISITED

Let's review the first few chapters of Genesis from a new perspective that incorporates the points I've been presenting in this book.

I tend to believe that the story of creation in the Bible is an extremely simplified and summarized version of the truth when properly interpreted. It's the same type of "truth" we tell children to explain things they don't know enough about to understand, such as where babies come from. Or trying to explain to a non-technically trained person how a computer works. While what we tell them is more or less true, it leaves out a vast amount of detail that they simply wouldn't understand without years of learning.

Likewise, with the biblical story of creation. The Sumerian story of creation (written over a thousand years earlier than Genesis) is essentially the same but includes a few more details than the Biblical version. But considering that even the Sumerian story was written thousands of years after the actual events, it shouldn't be surprising if it isn't exactly a perfect documentary of what actually happened. On a side note, it's interesting that the Sumerian texts also refer to a time before the Gods appeared, describing the earth as dark and watery, with no sunlight, moonlight, or vegetation.

There are two stories of creation in Genesis that have several similarities and differences. The first one is the seven "day" story. The second is a more detailed description of the creation of humans and the "garden" of Eden. If you look at the sequence of events in the first story, it matches the process of turning a lifeless planet into a living planet—a process we would call "terraforming" today. Scientists have done many studies on the possibility of terraforming Mars into an Earth-like planet. Interestingly, the steps involved follow the outline given in Genesis.

One thing to note in both creation stories in Genesis is that the earth already existed in some form at the beginning of each narrative. Neither story has a statement like "God said, 'Let there be an earth,' and there was an earth." That's because it was already there. In the first story, the earth starts as a water planet. There was no land. If we accept the current scientific view of how planets are formed, then a water world would be a very natural type of planet that would exist in what they call the "Goldilocks zone"—a distance from the sun where liquid water can exist, not too hot (too close) and not too cold (too far).

After the creation of "light," the next step in Genesis is creating an atmosphere. This is the first step scientists have taken in terraforming Mars. Using a variety of genetically engineered single-celled organisms like algae and bacteria, an atmosphere can be created that will support plants, animals, and humans. In Genesis, after the atmosphere was created, which separated the water above (clouds) and the waters below (ocean), the next step was to create dry land.

To create dry land on a water world would require the very careful "cracking" of the solid mantle of the planet. Cracking the mantel would allow portions to rise, creating dry land and oceans. I suspect that humans learning how to successfully "crack" a planet's mantle without blowing the whole planet apart will require a fair number of attempts and failures before we get it right. Apparently, the "Gods" successfully did it to the earth, so it's probably safe to say that earth wasn't their first attempt.

The next step in Genesis is the creation of plants. Notice we are seeing the development of what we call the "food chain." This would also be the next step in terraforming Mars.

The fourth step in Genesis is the creation of the sun, moon, and stars. I'll discuss this step and the first step later. For now, we'll continue with the fifth step: creating the marine life and birds. Since a breathable atmosphere and the foundation of the food chain (plants and micro-organisms) have already been created, larger life forms like brine shrimp, fish, and birds can now be added. Obviously, you would start with the smaller creatures and then add slightly larger ones that will eat the smaller ones, and so forth. Again, following the food chain.

The sixth step of Genesis is the addition of dry land creatures—first adding the ones that feed on plants and then the carnivores. You now have an Earth-like planet capable of supporting humans, which, according to Genesis, were also created during the sixth step or "day." It's important to point out that both male and female humans were created on this "day." It's also important to point out that the word translated as "man" in these verses (Genesis 1:26–27) is "Adam," used here to mean "humans," and it's also the same word used later as the name of the first man. In these verses, the word Adam is plural and used to mean "humans" since it refers to males and females.

While it might take quite a while before humans start terraforming Mars, I have no doubt that we eventually will. Technologically speaking, I'm fairly certain we could start the process now. We already can create genetically altered organisms, including humans, and we've been able to send spacecraft to Mars for quite some time. The only thing stopping us is a lack of will by our current governments. That will change, or some business entity or group of businesses will decide to do it on their own. Either way, it's going to happen sooner or later. The important point here is, if we can do it, does it really take that much imagination to believe that some technologically advanced race of beings terraformed the earth and created a genetically modified version of themselves thousands of years ago? For the intellectually honest, it shouldn't.

When reading the Bible, I think it's important to keep in mind a couple of inarguable facts, specifically, where Abraham grew up and where Moses grew up. Abraham grew up in the city of Ur, which was in Sumeria, which was in the current country of Iraq. He was born around 1996 BC. So, what do you think Abraham would have been taught growing up? I would tend to think he was taught what everyone else in his time believed, and we have a good idea of what those beliefs were based on the ancient Sumerian writings we have today.

Moses was born around 1392 BC and was raised in Egypt as the son of Pharoah's daughter. Being a grandson of the Pharaoh, it's safe to say he got a good education. So, what do you think Moses would have been taught growing up? He probably would have been taught what the Egyptians believed at the time. I'm sure he was also taught about Hebrew beliefs by his mother and others. I would recommend that you read the *Egyptian Book of the Dead*. It was written before Moses's time, and it will give you an idea of what Egyptians believed and some of what Moses was undoubtedly taught as Pharaoh's grandson.

It's also important to realize that Abraham and Moses lived after the flood, a cataclysmic event that destroyed the civilization(s) existing at the time. Civilizations that may have been as technologically advanced as we are. According to the Bible, the flood occurred about two thousand years after creation. There are stories of it in civilizations all over the world. Whether that two-thousand-year period is exactly correct or not doesn't matter. The important point is it happened a **long** time after the beginning of human history, and just as an all-out nuclear war would do now, it wiped out virtually all knowledge and records of history up to that time.

Of course, the people that survived would try to pass on as much knowledge as they could, but very little would survive, and even what little did survive would most likely wind up being in the extremely simplified and summarized type of stories we tell children.

Imagine our current society being destroyed by some cataclysmic event and only eight people survived. All of our infrastructure is destroyed and gone—no electricity, no computers, no mining, no metal production. Perhaps there would be some surviving items you could use for a while. Maybe some vehicles and fuel could be salvaged and used until they finally broke down and rusted away. But with only eight survivors, how long might it take to get oil wells and an oil refinery going again? I can pretty much guarantee it's not going to happen in the lifetime of those eight survivors. Do any of them even know how to drill for oil? Or build a refinery? Or mine for iron? Or build a smelter? Or generate electricity?

And even if they did record that information, how many generations do you think that knowledge would last considering they will be spending most of their time just finding and growing food, shelter, water, clothes? Humanity would be right back in the Stone Age. Now imagine parents trying to tell their children about cell phones and computers four hundred years later. "Our ancestors had machines made of glass, plastic, and iron that could talk, hear, and see." ("Excuse me, mommy, but what is plastic?") Never mind that the machines contained all of the information in the world. They were like magical little messengers with which you could instantly communicate with people anywhere on earth. And there were carts that had motors and could move by themselves, even ones that could fly like birds. And on and on. What do you think those stories would sound like five thousand years later?

This is what we are dealing with when we read writings that are thousands of years old, describing events that happened thousands of years before the writings were even written. Even worse, the writings were written by people that had no knowledge of, or experience with, the level of technology discussed in the stories. Of course, they sound like nonsensical magic! Fiery flying chariots that roared like thunder with wheels within wheels and "eyes" (lights?) all around them (Ezekiel 1). How would someone from even four hundred years ago describe a helicopter or a jet? Maybe like some magical flying chariot?

I'm sure Abraham taught his children the Sumerian stories that he had learned, and those stories were undoubtedly passed down through the generations to Moses. Moses learned those stories and had the benefit of learning whatever knowledge and stories Egypt possessed at the time. From those, he wrote down the two stories of creation we read in Genesis.

Christians like to believe that God dictated the first five books of the Bible, and Moses just wrote down what God said. This belief comes from Jewish oral history. Unfortunately, that's not what the Bible actually says. It **does** say that God gave the "law" (the Ten Commandments) to Moses. The actual Hebrew word used is "hatorah," which means "the law" and that is how the word is used throughout the Old Testament until we get to the Book of Nehemiah where, for the first time, Nehemiah used the word to refer to the entire Pentateuch (the first five books of the Bible) (see Nehemiah 8:2). Over time, it became common to refer to the Pentateuch as "the law," even though that was **not** the original meaning. Because the Bible **says that God gave Moses "the law," it became the traditional belief that** God gave Moses the entire Pentateuch, but that's not what the texts actually say.

Read Exodus 25:16, where God tells Moses to put the stone tablets of "the law" **inside the ark**. Then, read Deuteronomy 31:26, in which Moses commands the Levites to put the "Book of the Law" **beside the ark**. There is a difference between the stone tablets containing the Ten Commandments, which God wrote, and the Book of the Law, which Moses wrote. God's writings went **inside** the ark, and Moses' writings went **beside** the ark. Neither Moses nor God considered Moses' writings the same as God's writings.

Why is this important? Because it means that God **did not**, in fact, dictate the stories of creation to Moses. These are stories that Moses learned from somewhere else. Notice that to argue that God dictated the entire Pentateuch to Moses creates all sorts of issues with the writings that must be "explained away." Accepting that God authored the two tablets of stone and Moses wrote the rest doesn't create any issues with the writings. It creates issues for those who **want** to believe God wrote it all, but what people **want** to believe, or even what **most** people believe, doesn't make it true. What matters is, does it add up? Does the belief fit the facts? If it doesn't, it doesn't matter how many believe it; it still isn't true.

So, where did Moses get the stories of creation? My bet would be from the beliefs of the Sumerians passed down by Abraham and the beliefs of the Egyptians that he learned as the grandson of the Pharaoh.

I said earlier that I would talk more about creation's first and fourth steps later. The fourth step in Genesis is the creation of the sun, moon, and stars. It seems extremely odd that if creation was measured in literal days, the sun wouldn't be created until the fourth day. Logically, if the first thing created was light, you would think there would need to be some source for the light. The only source of light in the universe as we see it is our suns (stars). Furthermore, the spinning of the earth creates day and night as portions of it rotate into and out of the stream of light coming from the sun.

It's hard to see how you could have the first morning and evening, the first day, if the sun didn't exist. I suspect that the original story of creation got confused from when it was first explained to someone and when it was finally written down in Genesis. It's not hard to imagine that what was originally described as six steps or phases was later described as six days, and the "beginning" and "end" became the "morning" and "evening" and, hence, a day. You simply can't have what we call a "day" without the sun. Consequently, it makes no sense that the first three periods of the creation story would be called a "day."

The universe can be divided into two basic forms: energy and matter. As we know, energy and matter can be converted from one to the other. An atom bomb is the conversion of matter into energy, and while we haven't completely mastered it yet, scientists are currently creating electrons and positrons from photons (light)...i.e., creating matter from energy. Given what we know about physics, it's easy to understand that once you have energy, if you know how, you can create matter.

While there are many different frequencies of electromagnetic energy (microwaves, X-rays, etc.), the ones that humans can experience directly we call "light." Describing how the universe was created would logically and scientifically make sense that the first thing required would be energy. It would also make sense that if you were trying to explain this to someone unfamiliar with the electromagnetic spectrum, you could just use the term "light." That's something they would understand, and, if you're using the term "light" to represent all electromagnetic frequencies, it would be the truth. Hence, the first step of creation is the creation of light (energy).

Separating the "light" from the "darkness" could be one way of describing converting some of the energy to matter. The matter is "dark." You can only see it if it gives off electromagnetic energy such as infrared light (heat) or if light reflects off of it. Substituting energy for "light" and matter for "darkness" makes the first step of creation a logical and understandable statement. But it still doesn't provide a mechanism for calling it a "day."

Genesis 1:1 states, *"In the beginning, the Gods created the heavens and the earth."* That statement summarizes the "days" or steps that follow. If the earth were the whole point of creation, then it would make sense that the earth was the first body of matter to exist. Consequently, it would have been the original center point of the universe. A few years ago, a couple of scientists pointed out that if Earth **were** the center of the universe, there wouldn't be any need for dark matter or dark energy, both of which are scientific pixie dust made up to avoid facing the fact that Einstein's Theory of Relativity regarding gravity doesn't match the facts of what we observe in our solar system and the rest of the universe. So maybe our solar system is, in fact, the center of the universe, and everything else (stars, galaxies, etc.) was built around it.

Let's move on to the second story of creation in Genesis. I think it's important to note that in the first story of creation, the word translated as "God" is always Elohim (which means Gods). The second story, starting at Genesis 2:4, switches to using the term Lord God (Yahweh Elohim in Hebrew). In other words, it's now about a **particular** God; in this case, the same God (Yahweh) that later becomes the personal God of the Israelites.

Genesis 2:4–5 sets the stage for this second story of creation. You'll notice this story is **not** about the creation of the earth and the universe. There's no mention of a water world, making an atmosphere, making dry land, the sun, moon and stars, etc. That's all been done. This story is about the creation of the "garden" and humans.

An interesting statement is made at the end of Genesis 2:5: *"there was no man* (in Hebrew "Adam", i.e., humans) **to till the land**." If you stop and think about it, that statement provides the **reason** for creating humans: to "till the land"; i.e., to do the work. This correlates with the Sumerian creation story. In the Sumerian story, the Gods that were doing all of the manual labor decided they shouldn't have to do that type of work, so they went to the leaders and asked them to make a servant race to do the work. After considering the idea, the leaders agreed and assigned a particular God the task of creating the new slave race. In Sumerian, that God was Enki, which generally means "Lord of the Earth." He was called Ea by the Assyrians and Babylonians. An interesting side note is that starting around 1900 BC, he was occasionally referred to by the number forty, which was considered his "sacred number." Enki was the God in charge of the project to create a slave race, and he assembled a team of other Gods to help him.

To understand what the ancient writers are trying to tell us (both Moses and the Sumerians), you have to drop the childish idea of a magical being that just speaks and—poof! things appear. That's not reality; that's fantasy. In 1961, US President John Kennedy announced the goal of sending American astronauts to the moon. In 1969, the first men landed on the moon. So, we **could** say, "The President said, 'Let us send man to the moon,' and men went to the moon, and everyone saw it and said it was good." Although it is extremely simplified, that would essentially be a true statement.

Now imagine how that story might be told two thousand years after a cataclysmic event that sent mankind back to the Stone Age. The Great Magical One, the infinitely wise (knowledgeable) and all-powerful (technologically advanced) leader of the ancients said, "'Let us send a man to the moon' (something that would seem impossible to Stone

Age people) and men went to the moon, and all the Magical Ones saw that it was good." Again, from the perspective of people with virtually no technology, that statement is true. It's not difficult to see how the people hearing that story might imagine that the Great Magical One is endowed with supernatural powers, and he simply speaks and—poof!—it happens. But we know that's not how it works.

While that story would be true, it leaves out the details of eight years' worth of work (building on centuries worth of increasing scientific knowledge) by thousands of scientists, engineers, and workers that made it happen. This is **exactly** what has happened with the stories of creation being told, written down, and translated by technologically ignorant people over thousands of years. They became mythologized and turned into stories of supernatural magic. Because these stories have been believed to be supernatural (magical) for thousands of years, even though we now have a lot of technology, most "believers" still think of them as happening by some supernatural (magical) means. Paul the apostle said, *"When I was a child, I talked like a child, I reasoned like a child, I thought like a child. When I became a man, I put away those childish things"* (1 Corinthians 13:11). If you want to understand the truth, you have to stop that childish, magical, fantasy type of thinking.

Genesis 2:6 uses a word used only once in the Bible. The word in Hebrew is "we-ed." The "e" in the Hebrew "we" part is upside down, but I can't type it. It is normally translated as "mist" and describes how the ground was watered even though no rain had fallen yet. The word is a two-part word. The "ed" part does indeed mean mist. The "we" part makes it a particular **type** of mist. The *Brown-Driver-Briggs Hebrew Lexicon* associates the word with an Assyrian word, which can be translated to flood, mass of waters, and **overflow for irrigation**. I suspect this is one of those cases where the word's exact meaning was lost over time because it described something the translators had no experience of. If I asked you what would cause a "mist" to come out of the ground in my flower bed and water the flowers every night, I bet it wouldn't take long to guess what it was: a **sprinkler**! Genesis states this happened before any shrub or plant had yet sprouted on the "earth." The word for "earth" is also the word for "ground," and I would make the case that what the text is talking about is the ground that is going to be used for the "garden."

When you read about all the different types of plants and trees that were in the "garden" and consider the fact that animals and humans lived ***in*** the "garden," it should be clear that the "garden" was pretty big. The use of the word "garden" is misleading. At least as we understand the meaning of the word today. Unless we're talking about the thirty-nine-acre gardens of Buckingham Palace, we think of a garden as a little patch of ground in the backyard. Certainly, it is nothing big enough that we would expect humans to live in it. We also don't generally plant trees in a garden. The Hebrew word translated as "garden" also means "enclosure" or "enclosed garden." So, the "garden" was surrounded by some sort of barrier or wall. For that matter, it's possible that it could have been entirely enclosed. What we are reading about is something that we would call a farm today. Considering the size of the "garden" and the "mist" that came out of the ground to water it, I think a far more accurate understanding of Genesis 2:6 would be that God put in a sprinkler system to water the farm before he planted anything in it—just as we would do today.

Genesis 2:7 states that God formed/fashioned man, using the dust/clay/mud of the ground/earth. In the Sumerian texts, the Gods mixed "clay" with the flesh and blood of one of the Gods to create humans. They also state that they created man "in their image." I keep referring to the Sumerian texts because of how closely they match what we read in Genesis, the fact that many of them are much older than Genesis, and for the additional details that they contain. It's quite obvious that the Sumerian writings and Genesis are simply different writings referring to the same historical events. The Sumerian writings are what Abraham was taught and which he undoubtedly passed on to his children and their children—all the way down to Moses. The fact that mud or clay is mentioned in both stories is not a coincidence. What we read as "mud" or "clay" can also be understood as the elements of the earth.

As far as we know, the basic elemental table is consistent throughout the universe. Individual planets and stars, however, consist of different percentages of those elements. The Gods were obviously masters of genetic manipulation. Genetic code is simply biological programming (software). It's the genetic code that determines, at a minimum, the physical characteristics of an organism. When we consider the vast array of life forms on Earth, there can't be any doubt that whoever designed them were experts in genetic coding. Human biology is intimately linked to the solar cycle, gravity, and magnetic fields of the earth and the moon. While the earth may have been designed for humans, it's also true that humans were designed for the earth's environment. I think Genesis 2:7 is telling us that the Gods created humans by modifying their own genetic code ("in their image, and after their likeness") and combining it with, and designing it for, the elements of earth (the "mud" or "clay").

While some people will object to the idea of humans being a genetically modified version of the Gods, there's another major fact in the history of humans and Gods that I think proves that it's true. The animal kingdom is divided into groups that we call species. One of the aspects of a species is that animals within a species can interbreed, but they can't interbreed with animals from a different species. Even though the various sub-species within a species may not ever crossbreed naturally, they can be interbred by artificial means. For example, cougars don't breed with house cats. But by using artificial insemination, we can create a crossbreed of a house cat and a cougar, or a house cat with any other type of cat. But we can't crossbreed any member of the cat species with any member of the dog species. The genetic coding is simply not compatible.

The Bible and writings from virtually all other ancient civilizations have stories of humans and Gods mating and having offspring. The offspring were generally legendary kings or great heroes, such as Nimrod in the Bible, and the Greek heroes Hercules, Achilles, Perseus, and many others.

Genesis 6:1–4 states that the "Sons of God" (Benai-Elohim in Hebrew) mated with the "daughters of man," and their offspring were known as the "Nephilim." The Nephilim were the "mighty men of old, men of renown." It is commonly believed that the word "Nephilim" comes from the root word "Naphal," which means "to fall," so they say that Nephilim means "the fallen ones."

But when the Old Testament was translated into the Greek Septuagint, the word Nephilim was translated as "Gigantes," which means "Earth-born." Nothing like "to fall" or "fallen," for which there are certainly Greek words. The definition of "Earth-born" fits with the concept presented in the verses. These beings were the result of the "Sons of God" (**not** Earth-born) mating with human women (definitely Earth-born). Referring to them as Earth-born makes sense. They were descendants of the Gods (sky-born) and humans (beings created on and for earth) and were born on earth.

As with other verses that don't fit the modern Christian dogma, Christian leaders make up convoluted explanations as to why these verses don't mean what they clearly say. Other than these verses, the term "sons of God" is used three other times in the Old Testament—all in Job. In every one of those other verses, everyone agrees that the term is referring to angels. (As I've pointed out before, the Hebrew words translated as "angels" are the same words translated as "Gods" or "God.") There is no justification to believe that the term "Sons of God" in Genesis 6:1–4 doesn't mean exactly what it means every other time it is used. Most Christians just don't like the idea of what it implies. Specifically, that the Gods and "angels" are **not** some sort of magical, non-physical (spiritual) beings. Since they clearly bred with humans, they are obviously physical beings.

The author of the New Testament book of Jude states that he is "a servant of Jesus Christ and brother of James." The James referred to is understood to be James, the brother of Yeshua (Jesus). One of the twelve disciples was named Jude as well as one of Yeshua's brothers. If the author of Jude was the brother of James, who was a brother of Yeshua, then he would also have been Yeshua's brother and may have been Jude the disciple as well. In any case, the book of Jude is one of the books accepted as part of the Christian Holy Bible.

The interesting thing here is that Jude 1:14–15 is a direct quote from Enoch 1:9. The book of Enoch was well known at the time of Yeshua and was considered one of the Holy books by the early Christians, but it didn't get included when the Bible as we know it was put together. It **did** get included in the Ethiopian Bible, and obviously Jude thought the book of Enoch was valid enough to quote it to help prove his case against certain Christians he considered ungodly. If you read the book of Enoch (and I would encourage you to do so), you will see why it wasn't included in the Bible by the Catholic church. A fair amount of Christian dogma would have to be thrown out if the book of Enoch was included. On the other hand, unlike the Old Testament, a lot of the Messianic themes of the New Testament are included in Enoch.

The first part of the Book of Enoch describes what it calls the "Watchers" (Sons of God, angels). The Watchers became infatuated with human women and decided to descend to Earth (from wherever they were) and take human women as wives. It's the same story as in Genesis 6:1–4 but with far more detail. The Book of Enoch even names the leaders of the Watchers and states that there was a total of two hundred Watchers that all joined in with the plan to take human wives. If the Book of Enoch had been included in the Bible, there couldn't be any argument that the "sons of God" in Genesis 6:1–4 were not, in fact, Elohim (gods/angels).

All of the points I've outlined above provide undeniable proof that humans are part of the same species as the Gods. If they weren't, based on what we know from the animal kingdom, humans and Gods wouldn't be able to interbreed. The fact that they do also tells me that the Gods are not some magical apparitions, ghosts, or spirits. They are physical beings just like we are. But just as a house cat is not the same as a leopard, even though they are the same species, likewise the "Gods" undoubtedly designed humans to be inferior to themselves. The original humans were designed to be the servant race, after all. On a sidenote, humans and our supposed evolutionary ancestors (monkeys) can **not** be interbred.

One last observation on the resistance of modern Christians to the idea of humans and Gods interbreeding. The **entire concept** of Christianity is based on the belief that Yeshua was the "son of God" **and** "the son of man"; i.e., a crossbreed. Mary had to get that Y chromosome from somewhere, and if Yeshua was truly a "son of God," then it had to have come from a God. While they've made up a magical mythical "miracle" to explain Mary's "virgin" birth, it is just more of that childish fantasy-style storytelling that defines much of modern Christianity. If they truly want to believe Yeshua was half-God and half-human, then they need to accept the unavoidable truth that Mary was impregnated by a "God," which means Gods can, and do, interbreed with humans.

For years, I wondered how it was that whenever any of the Biblical characters saw one of the Gods, they instantly recognized them as Gods. The Gods don't actually have wings like the angels that people have painted and sculpted for centuries. If you do some reading, you will find that the only time Biblical persons saw winged beings was when they were seeing them in a dream or vision. In all of the cases in the Bible where they were awake and not in a vision, the Gods did **not** have wings. They looked like men, yet somehow, people knew they weren't just ordinary men.

The answer came to me after reading the Book of Enoch. While I'm not claiming that the stories in Enoch are absolutely true, it did provide a clue as to how the Biblical characters recognized the Gods. Chapter 106 of Enoch tells the story of the birth of Noah. As it puts it, *"His body was white as snow and red as the bloom of a rose, and the hair of his head was white as wool, and his eyes were beautiful."* When his father, Lamech saw his new baby boy, Lamech was afraid of him. So Lamech ran and told his father, Methuselah, that he had fathered a child that was *"unlike a man, but similar to the **children of the angels of heaven**."* He also told Methuselah that he didn't think the child was his but was *"from the angels"*; i.e., a child of one of the Gods.

The key that provided the answer to my wondering was that Noah was **white** and his father thought he was like the Gods/angels. Up until then, people were darker skinned and had dark hair and eyes. But the Gods/angels were white. This is why the

Biblical characters instantly recognized they weren't just regular human men. Now, before anyone goes off on some racist tangent, that isn't the point. I'm simply stating a fact as it was recorded in Enoch. If that fact happens to offend you, well, frankly, that's your personal problem.

Mistaking white people for Gods the first time they saw them happened repeatedly in dark-skinned cultures around the world. It's one of the reasons the Spaniards were able to rob the South Americans of their gold when they first discovered the Americas, because of old stories of **white** Gods that the South Americans had encountered in the past. Since the Spaniards were white, the South Americans assumed they too must be Gods.

Meanwhile, back in Genesis, after creating the man, "*The Lord God took the man and put him in the Garden of Eden* **to work it and take care of it**" (Genesis 6:15). This verse reinforces Genesis 2:5 (and the Sumerian texts) regarding the **purpose** of creating mankind; i.e., to **work** the farm so the Gods wouldn't have to do it themselves—not exactly the modern Christian view.

Modern Christianity imagines the Garden of Eden as Paradise. Where does this idea come from? How do you go from "enclosed" and "garden" (the actual meaning of the Hebrew word "gan") to *par-*

adise? Well, if we trace the origin of the Greek word "paradeisos," which is translated into English as "paradise," we find that it comes from a Persian origin: "pairi-daeza" or "pardis," meaning "garden" or "walled enclosure" or "orchard," which sounds like the "enclosed garden" we read about in Genesis. The misconstruing of the word happened when the New Testament was being written. The term paradeisos was used to refer to the wondrous new dwelling place, which would be the future reward of the righteous (heaven). From there, the word's new meaning was then retrofitted to the original Garden of Eden, turning it into a paradise. This is another example of revisionist history.

Nothing in the Old Testament states the Garden of Eden was a paradise. Or that nothing ever died there. Modern Christianity views the Garden of Eden as an idyllic place where Adam and Eve just strolled around eating fruit, smelling the roses, and petting the lions when they weren't basking on the beach sipping fruit drinks. That's just pure fantasy. They were created for and put on the farm (garden) to **work it**; that means doing the labor and weeding it, trimming it, planting and pruning the trees, harvesting, and all the other work that must be done on a farm. And nowhere does the Old Testament claim that nothing ever died there. That, too, is pure fantasy. If nothing had ever died, the place would have been overrun with mice, rats, cats, bugs, and bacteria. Furthermore, if nothing ever died, the warning to Adam not to eat of the tree of the knowledge of good and evil **lest he die** wouldn't have meant anything to Adam. How would he know what **death** was? Why would he be afraid of that?

In Genesis 2:18, Yahweh said, *"It is not good that man should be alone; I will make a helper for him."* After Adam named all of the animals (when did Adam learn how to talk?), verse twenty mentions that for Adam, *"no suitable helper was found."* So, God put Adam to sleep, took one of his ribs, and then closed up the wound (verse 21). Stop and think about this for a minute. That sounds an awful lot like a surgical procedure. Why would God need a rib from Adam to make Eve? Why didn't he just use the clay to form Eve and breathe life into her like he did with Adam? Better yet, why didn't he just say, "Let there be woman"—and poof!—Eve appears like the sun, moon, and stars? What's with all this physical messing around with surgery and ribs? All these mundane physical processes that sound like things we do today? The author is just giving us a little more detail about how things happened—and it wasn't by magic. It should be a hint and a wake-up call for the believers of a supernatural God speaking things into existence in some fantasy land.

Then He made a woman from the rib He had taken from Adam and brought her to him (Genesis 2:22). You will notice that wherever God made Eve, it wasn't where Adam was, because He "brought her to him." Since we aren't using magic, creating a woman from a rib will require some sort of hospital or lab. Maybe Adam was already back on the farm by the time Eve was finished, or perhaps he was just in another room down the hall, still recuperating from surgery.

You'll also notice that it doesn't say how long it was from when God took the rib until he presented Eve. On the other hand, in the first creation story of Genesis, the man and woman were created on the same "day." It must have been an exhausting day for Adam. Getting created, being put in the "garden," getting warned not to eat from a certain tree, naming all the animals, then being put to sleep and having a rib taken out—all in one day. It makes me feel tired just writing about it. Apparently, it made God tired as well, so He took Saturday off. 😌

I'd like to take a minute now to discuss the creation of Adam. According to the Bible, God formed him out of the dirt and then breathed into him the breath of life, and—poof—he became a living being. Then, he supposedly did everything mentioned above on the first day of his life. Think for a moment. What's a baby like when it's born? Can it talk? Walk? Think? No! It takes around a year to learn how to walk—a year to two years to begin talking and many more years to truly begin being able to think. And yet supposedly, Adam and Eve could do all those things instantly, the first day they were "born." Does that make any sense?

Here again, I find the ancient Sumerian writings a bit more helpful. In the story of "Enki and Ninmah," the Goddess Namma (interestingly close to mamma) kneads some clay, places it in her womb, and gives birth to the first humans. In other Sumerian writings, a God is killed, and then his blood is mixed with clay, which was used to create the first humans. Some of the stories mention "birth gods," female gods that were used as what we would call "surrogate" mothers today. Just as we do today, the human eggs were implanted in the "birth gods," and then they carried and gave birth to the humans.

The Sumerian writings provide enough details to interpret what the Biblical story has greatly shortened and mythologized. Today, we create modified creatures using the same process the Sumerian texts allude to. We modify the DNA of the creature's egg and then implant it in the female creature's womb to grow until birth. What's important here is that the methodology the Sumerian texts describe is exactly what we would do today if we wanted to create a race of modified humans! How is it that a Stone Age civilization could just accidentally "make up" a story that describes our modern-day process of genetic modification, artificial insemination, and surrogacy? If it was just fantasy, why would they mention "mixing blood and clay" and "birth mothers"? I don't believe it's just a coincidence. Even though the story has been shortened, simplified, and even confused, a thinking person can still recognize what it's about. And if we can modify creatures today, is it really that hard to believe that some "gods" did it thousands of years ago?

The Sumerian texts also state that the first humans could not procreate on their own. This is another tactic that we would probably use today if we created some genetically modified creature. Initially make it incapable of reproduction until we tested it in our environment and made sure it performed as we expected. Once we were confident that it "fit" without messing things up, we would then make it capable of reproducing on its own. So, after a while, the "gods" modified the humans to enable them to create and bear their own offspring. Perhaps that is when "god" commanded them to "be fruitful and multiply."

For me, this interpretation of the Sumerian writings makes the Bible believable. The "gods" created humans by genetically modifying their DNA ("in our image, in our likeness"), then implanting the modified eggs/embryos into female "gods" who carried them until birth. Adam and Eve (males and females) were born, trained, and raised as the servants of the "gods" and then put to work in the "garden" of Eden. (The Sumerian texts also state that the gods planted a garden of Eden.) Finally, the "gods" gave the new creatures the ability to reproduce on their own.

Genesis 3 is the story of the "deceiving" serpent, the eating of the fruit, being punished, and getting kicked out of the garden. I want to make a couple of points here. The modern image of the serpent is of a snake in a tree. But that obviously has to be wrong. There would be no point in God condemning the serpent to crawl on its belly and eat dust for the rest of its life if that's what it already did anyway. So, the serpent wasn't like the snakes we know today.

Also, how is it that Eve wasn't shocked at having some creature speak to her? Had she not been in the "garden" long enough to realize that animals don't talk? Or did all the animals talk at that time? Or, if we want to go out there, could the humans communicate telepathically with the animals? I've read stories of Native Americans speaking to "spirit guides" that appear as animals. And South American shamans claim the plants tell them how to make their medicines—in both cases, generally, after ingesting some hallucinogenic plant of some kind. Maybe hallucinogens open our eyes, ears, and telepathic abilities.

There is another possibility considered, one that could also explain what actually happened when the Gods "confused their languages" (Genesis 11:7) at Babel. Maybe, up until Babel, humans had the ability to communicate telepathically. Perhaps they could communicate to a certain degree with the animals. That could explain why Eve wasn't shocked and didn't run screaming when the serpent "spoke" to her. It could also explain why people suddenly couldn't communicate when God "confused" their language at Babel.

I've always found it odd that archeologists haven't found any writings from before the flood. It could be that, like us, they were technologically advanced enough that they didn't need to store information on paper or clay tablets. All of their information might have been stored digitally on some sort of devices like our computers. When the flood destroyed their civilization, all that technology would have been lost, and just a few hundred years after the flood, no one would have known or recognized what those devices were, much less how to use them if they still existed. Or, it could be that having telepathic abilities, they simply didn't need to keep written records. I'm not claiming this is exactly what happened, but it would explain a few things.

It's interesting that the earliest writings were all based on "pictures," like Egyptian hieroglyphs and Chinese writings. Mental images, "pictures," would be the most natural form of communicating information telepathically. We've all heard the saying "a picture is worth a thousand words." That's true. A picture can instantly convey a meaning that would otherwise require a whole lot of words to describe. Although the flood would have wiped out all technology, if the people before the flood had used some kind of symbol-based written language (like our alphabetic-based languages), that written language would **not** have been lost due to the flood. Noah and his family would all have known it and would have used and preserved it.

It's also interesting to note that humans can communicate telepathically when talking to the Gods in a dream or when having a vision. That's how most of the prophets in the Bible communicated with God. People who claim to have communicated with "aliens" also state that the communication happens telepathically. So, it would seem that humans have the ability, but we don't know how to use it on our own. Again, just a theory, but maybe that's what happened at Babel. The Gods somehow took away humans' ability to communicate telepathically.

In any case, Eve had a conversation with the "serpent" and wound up eating the forbidden fruit. The Sumerian texts also have a story of the first man missing out on immortality. In his case, it wasn't because he ate the forbidden fruit, but because he **didn't** eat the food that would have made him immortal when it was offered to him. The reason he didn't eat it was because one of the Gods had warned him not to eat any food the other Gods might offer him because the food would kill him. It's interesting that both stories involve deception, food, and the threat of dying if you eat the food.

Something I find interesting in Eve's conversation with the serpent that supposedly deceived her is that if you look at what the serpent told her, the Bible confirms that everything it said was true. In Genesis 3:4–5, the serpent said, *"You will not certainly die, for the Gods know that **the day** you eat from it your eyes will be opened and you will be like the Gods knowing good and evil."* Since Genesis tells us the humans were kicked out of the "garden" and then had children and lived several hundred years more, they obviously didn't die **the day** they ate the fruit. Contrast that with Genesis 2:16–17, where Yahweh tells the man, *"From any tree of the garden you may freely eat, but from* *the tree of the knowledge of good and evil you shall not eat, for **in the day** that you eat from it you will surely die."*

Here is where modern Christians suddenly want to claim that **the day** was not twenty-four hours. To heck with the six literal days of creation. They make up all sorts of convoluted explanations to try to explain away why Adam and Eve didn't die **the day** they ate the fruit when, in fact, that's exactly what they were told would happen. But the important thing to notice is that the serpent told the truth! They didn't die **the day** they ate the forbidden fruit. In fact, they wouldn't have died, period, except for the fact that God threw them out of the "garden" so that they wouldn't be able to eat from the Tree of Life!

In Genesis 3:22, Yahweh says, *"Behold, the man has become like one of Us, knowing good and evil, he must not be allowed to reach out his hand and also take from the tree of life and eat and live forever."* So, God drove them out of the "garden" and then, to make sure they didn't get back in, he put a "cherubim" with a "flaming sword" to guard the entrance. Again, the important thing to notice is that in Genesis 3:22, God verifies that what the serpent said was true: *"the man has become like one of Us, knowing good and evil"* and that if they didn't do something about it, there was a chance that the humans might also live forever. It should be quite apparent that eating the fruit itself was **not** the cause of their mortality. As God stated, had they not been prevented from eating from the Tree of Life, they would not only have the knowledge of good and evil but would have been immortal as well. Exactly **why** being immortal and knowing good and evil is fine for the Gods but not the humans is never explained.

You can certainly argue that the serpent tempted Eve and talked her into disobeying God's only rule, but you can't claim that it lied to her. That simply isn't true. If you wanted to be a real stickler, you could point out that apparently, God was a little less than truthful when He said that they would die **the day** they ate the fruit.

Something else I've always found interesting about this story is that when questioned, Adam excuses himself by blaming Eve. Then Eve defends herself by blaming the serpent. But when it was the serpent's turn, God didn't ask it why or allow it to offer any explanation or defense. Just as they have turned the "garden" into paradise, modern Christianity has retroactively turned the serpent into the Devil. As I pointed out earlier, there was no Devil in the Old Testament. The closest you can find is when someone (and multiple people were) identified as **a satan**. The Hebrew word means adversary, accuser. It was used just as we use "prosecutor" today—as a title, not a name. Some people will believe that I'm trying to defend the Devil. I've heard plenty of Christian preachers tell their parishioners that the Devil wants them to believe he doesn't exist, and therefore anyone that tries to tell them that the Devil doesn't exist is just an evil servant of the Devil. Notice the clever deceit they're preaching: anyone who tells you the truth that the Devil doesn't exist is a servant of the Devil!

Believing that there is a Devil provides a handy excuse for sinners. It's not their fault! The Devil made them do it. And because it's not their fault, there's nothing they need to change. Sure, they need to ask for forgiveness, but they're not a bad person. In America, we've seen this type of argument being pushed by liberals for a long time. They argue that the murderer shouldn't be executed because they were abused as a child, or were bullied, or were poor. In other words, it's not really the murderer's fault. It's the parents' fault, or their classmates' fault, or society's fault—or the Devil's fault. They use the same type of logic to defend thieves, drug addicts, alcoholics, and pedophiles.

It's the same argument that both Eve and Adam were trying to use: blame someone else. If you really believe the Devil exists, then think about this: Why would you ever discipline your child for misbehaving since they only did it because the Devil made them do it? It's not their fault! I will simply point out that the God in the "garden" didn't buy that argument, and neither should we. It's only by taking responsibility or being held responsible that people find the motivation to change.

On a little sidenote, although Yahweh Himself never uses the excuse, when it comes to evil, modern Christianity has adopted the same tactic Eve tried: blame someone else. In spite of the fact that Yahweh clearly states in Isaiah 45:7 that **He** creates both good and evil, that doesn't fit with what they want to believe, so they blame the Devil for the evil in the world. Of course, they will also argue that the Devil can only do what God allows him to do. But then they throw that out the window by explaining that God **has** to allow the Devil to do his evil deeds since Adam and Eve sinned and made the Devil the ruler of Earth. And then they tell you God is in complete control. If you can follow and make that logic work, congratulations; you're better than I am. Apparently even better than Yahweh himself since you can't find anywhere in the Bible where He states that or uses that reasoning.

The only way you can read the Devil into the serpent is if you already believe the serpent was the

Devil. Which is not what either the author of Genesis, nor the people living at the time Genesis was written, believed. You certainly can't get that belief from the actual words in Genesis. It simply isn't there. If the author had meant for the serpent to be identified as the Devil, he would have used that word himself. Or at least he would have used the word "Satan," but he doesn't. He doesn't because it wasn't.

Many writers over the last few centuries have noticed and pointed out the development of the concept of the Devil over the last few millennia. They've also pointed out that it **wasn't** a belief of people prior to that. That belief is simply a part of the mythologized narrative that has developed within modern Christianity.

The author of the Pentateuch wasn't trying to create a religion or make up a mystical story of the origins of humankind. He was simply trying to write down the actual **history** as he understood it. And that is exactly what he did. We go from creation to Yahweh calling Abraham out of his homeland (Sumeria) by Chapter 12. According to Christians, that's covering a roughly 2,700-year period of time—in eleven short chapters. Obviously, the author wasn't trying to write an exposition (a detailed, comprehensive explanation) of those 2,700 years. He was just setting the stage for the main story of the Old Testament, which is the history of the Israelites. For us to have any hope of learning the truth about the origins of humanity, we have to understand and accept that simple fact.

CHAPTER 8

WHAT IS THE TRUTH

The truth is, we don't have enough information to know **exactly** what the truth is. But there **is** enough evidence available to determine that the "official" stories are not true. They simply don't fit the facts. As I've pointed out throughout this book, when it comes to modern Christianity, the "official" positions regarding the inerrancy, accuracy, translation, authorship, and even the history of the Bible simply don't match the facts available to anyone that cares to look. Furthermore, I described earlier in the book how you can test the "promises" in the New Testament and determine for yourself whether they are true or not.

As I've said before, those that honestly, intelligently seek the truth will slowly learn that most of what they've been taught and almost everything that is published by the major information organizations today is actually not the truth. That includes everything from archeology to economics to physics to religion. You can pretty much bet that the "official" story or theory is not in fact the truth. At the same time as the "officials" are constantly pumping out propaganda, they are viciously attacking and destroying anyone that dares to disagree with them and tell the truth.

Before I present my current beliefs on this shared experience we call "reality," I'd like to go over some of those "official" stories. For example, the "official" story of how the universe came to exist is known as the Big Bang Theory. But if you bother researching the facts and evidence, you will find plenty of evidence proving that story is false. Of course, rarely will you find any of those contrary facts and evidence in any "official" publication. And if you do, you will notice they most often follow it up with denials by other "experts" and then attack and try to destroy whoever it was that published the truth in the first place. This is an intentional tactic. They will publish something that is true and then attack it with a massive amount of propaganda. The goal is to let people hear the truth but then discredit it so that the ignorant and uninformed will believe the truth is actually false. Sadly, that tactic is quite successful.

Let's assume for a moment that the Big Bang Theory is true. If that were the case, then there couldn't possibly have been any life forms of any type in the early universe since the conditions of the early universe would have instantly annihilated any organic matter. So how did life begin? If you spend a little time learning the most basic requirements of the simplest life forms—single-cell organisms—you will find that they must have a cell membrane that separates them from the outside world. They have to have DNA. The simplest life form has over 1 million base pairs of DNA. If even one of those base pairs is "wrong," the organism will fail to develop. It simply won't function. In addition to a cell membrane and DNA, single-cell organisms also have RNA and other molecular "components" (things like ribosomes, cytoplasm, mitochondria, flagellum, organelles, etc.) that enable them to function and reproduce. Without those other "components," they couldn't function. Or, in other words, they would not be alive. This combination of various components that are required for a functioning organism creates what is called "irreducible complexity."

Irreducible complexity simply means the absolute minimum components necessary for a system to function. If we consider a single piston internal combustion engine, we can identify the absolute minimum components necessary for it to function—things like a crankcase, crankshaft, cylinder wall, piston, connecting rod, intake and exhaust ports, spark plug, carburetor or fuel injector, electricity, and fuel. If you eliminate **any single one** of those components, the engine simply cannot function. The same is true for any cell of any type of organism. The only difference is that a single-piston internal combustion engine is orders of magnitude simpler than any cell. One microbiologist has said that the internal components and operation of a cell make the most sophisticated factory look like child's play in comparison.

To help put this in perspective, several years ago, genetic scientists created the first functioning organism whose DNA had been manually assembled by humans. The DNA consisted of approximately one million base pairs. Their first attempt at replacing the DNA of the single-celled organism they were working with failed. After analyzing what went wrong, they found that they had made a mistake on a **single base pair**. After correcting that base pair, they again replaced the DNA in one of the organisms, and this time it worked.

But the only real achievement here was the manual assembly of a million base pair DNA. And even then, they didn't actually "design" the DNA. Instead, they compared the DNA of the organism they were using with the DNA of several very closely related organisms and then copied what they believed was the bare minimum of the DNA base pairs. While that was a success, it also showed how difficult it would be for any "natural" formation of the simplest DNA. A single wrong base pair out of one million (1 of 1,000,000), and the organism died. Furthermore, they simply replaced the existing DNA of the organism with the one they had assembled. They didn't create the cell wall, RNA, ribosomes, cytoplasm, mitochondria, flagellum, organelles, or any of the other critical components of the single-celled organism.

A nucleotide consists of three parts: a phosphate, a sugar, and a nitrogen base. Evolutionists would have you believe that on a completely lifeless planet, nucleotides somehow randomly assembled themselves into a million base pair DNA (and that's ignoring how the phosphate, sugar, and nitrogen base might have formed in the first place). Then you're supposed to believe that the cell wall (composed of a specific mix of complex chemicals) just assembled itself. And then it was filled with (or formed around) the exact chemical fluid required for the cell to function. And then all of the many other absolutely essential cellular components just accidentally formed simultaneously, and the cell became a living, reproducing organism.

Do **just a little** research on the various components of a cell and the functions they perform, and then see for yourself if you can believe that all of those things just accidentally, randomly assembled themselves and then combined all at once into a functioning organism. If you have any reasoning ability at all, you simply won't be able to believe that.

When I was in grade school, the theory of evolution taught that life began by "spontaneous generation" when the first single-cell organisms "formed" in the "primordial mud" of the earth "millions of years ago." Since then, evolutionists have had to backtrack and modify their "theory" to eliminate the portions that science has proven impossible, one of those being spontaneous generation. Today evolutionists proclaim that the Theory of Evolution "does not provide an explanation for the origin of life" and "evolution, in fact, **is not the study of origins at all**," which is really interesting since they teach it to explain the origin of humans.[17]

---

[17] Justin W. Rice et al., "The Theory of Evolution Is Not an Explanation for the Origin of Life," *Evolution: Education and Outreach* 3 (April 2020), 141–142, https://doi.org/10.1007/s12052-010-0225-1.

In other words, they just ignore the most critical part. All of the evidence to date proves that life simply could not have begun by any "natural" process. Billions of dollars and thousands of careers have been spent trying to come up with some method by which life could have begun "naturally"—all to no avail, not to mention a complete waste of time and money. In fact, the majority of biological scientists do not believe in evolution. They have enough knowledge of the facts to know that spontaneous generation and evolution are impossible. But they can't publicly state that. If they do, they will never get another dime of government funding (where 90+ percent of all scientific funding comes from); in most cases, they will lose their job and be publicly scorned and denounced. The same scenario is true in many other areas of science, such as physics. Any physicist that questions Einstein's theory of relativity will suffer the same fate as any biologist or archeologist that questions the Theory of Evolution.

For the rational truth seeker, just recognizing what happens to anyone that questions the "official" position should tell you whether the "official" position is true or not. The truth doesn't need to be defended by those types of tactics. This is exactly what the Catholic church did for 1,500 years: kill the "heretics." The truth can usually be proven quite easily and clearly, without argument or long and complex "explanations." The real truth is that the only people who actually **believe** in the big bang theory and evolution are those that don't know enough about physics or biology to realize those theories simply don't match the facts.

So back to the question of how life began. If it couldn't have happened "naturally," how did we get here? The only possible answer is that ***it didn't happen "naturally."*** In other words, it was **caused** to happen. And to be **caused**, some sort of intelligence had to cause it, which leads to the explanation known as intelligent design. Evolutionists hate intelligent design because to them it means creation as described by the Bible. They're not bright enough to realize that creation as described by the Bible is not the only possible version of intelligent design. Intelligent design is the ***only*** possible explanation for life in the universe. But it gets even worse. As a number of scientists have recognized since the big bang theory was introduced, the big bang theory itself requires an initial **miracle** and then intelligent design to be able to result in the universe as we see it today. In other words, given the laws of physics, the universe as it is could not have happened "naturally"; it ***had to have been designed***.

But Christians are just as bad as evolutionists. Since the universe and life had to have been created by design, they claim that their mythologized version of the story of Biblical creation is true. Unfortunately, it doesn't. They make the same mistake as evolutionists: black-and-white thinking style (i.e., there's only two possible answers).

Just because it had to be designed and caused by an intelligence doesn't mean it was done by some all-powerful, all-knowing magical being they call "God." In fact, as I've already pointed out, that's not even what the Bible itself claims. Again, the original Hebrew word "Elohim," translated as "God" today, is actually a plural form of the word El, meaning multiple El's or "Gods"...i.e., more than one. To the people that actually knew them, the "Gods" were powerful, superior beings that ruled the world. The Sumerians, Akkadians, Assyrians, and Babylonians called them Anunnaki, which basically means sky gods. From our modern perspective, the "Gods" can be understood as beings that possessed vastly advanced technology compared to the ancient people of Earth.

The point here is that even according to the Bible, a **group of beings** created our universe. Whether they were "Gods" or computer programmers creating a virtual reality, the end result is still the same: intelligent design.

OK, let's get back to **how did life begin**? Based on the Bible and Sumerian writings, my perspective of the "Gods" is that they are/were humanoids that terraformed the earth and genetically engineered humans so they would have a servant race to work for them. They couldn't have come from Earth since it wasn't a habitable planet when they started changing it. But even if you accept my interpretation of what Genesis, the Sumerian texts, and other ancient writings say, it still doesn't explain the origin of life. While it could be the story of the beginning of humans, that just moves the problem one step away. Since the "Gods" seemingly live in this universe, where did they come from?

You also see this issue with evolutionists today. One of their latest concoctions is that the origin of life on Earth was bacteria or some other single-celled organisms that hitched a ride on asteroids from somewhere else. They are just pushing the annoying fact that there's no way life could have spontaneously occurred one step and millions of years away.

Genesis and all other creation myths, regardless of how bizarre the details of their myths might be, all agree on one basic point: the universe and humans were created by some intelligent beings, occasionally one but usually at least two or more. From all the information I've been able to accumulate, I'd have to agree with that basic premise. So, how can we put that premise into an explanation that fits with all the knowledge we have today?

The conclusion I finally came to, which is now rapidly gaining adherents in the scientific community, is that our entire universe is a virtual reality. It's called the simulation theory. Based on what I've learned about physics, biology, consciousness, and even religion, it's the **only** explanation that fits all of the facts that I'm aware of. For Christians, it explains how "heaven" is the "true" reality and our universe is just the "physical" (i.e., "not true") reality.

It also solves the problem of how life began in our universe. It didn't "just happen" by some "natural" mechanism. That is impossible. All the life forms we see were designed by whoever created the simulation. They are not a "natural" occurrence nor the result of any "evolution." Living organisms **are adaptable** within the limits of their DNA. So, we see variations created by external factors. For example, there is a wide variety of dogs that humans have created through selective breeding—variation, but not evolution. Although there are variations, the basic design of the life forms we see is how they were designed. That's why there aren't any "intermediate forms" or "missing links" that evolution requires but can't find.

You might wonder why I would consider ancient writings if I believe our universe is just a simulation. It's because even the simulation had to have had a beginning. Whether Earth was the primary purpose of the simulation or is just a habitable planet that some "gods" terraformed for their use much later doesn't matter. It had to have been designed and populated somehow. It wouldn't make sense to create the earth and start putting "players" (humans) on it that had no idea how to survive here. Remember, we are born completely ignorant. The first humans would have needed someone to nurture and teach them how to survive here—what to eat, what not to eat, how to build shelters, start fires, etc. According to the ancient texts, that's the function the "gods" performed.

In a universe as incomprehensibly massive as ours, many civilizations could have been progressing for a very long time. Earth could just be part of the expansion of one of those civilizations. Or it could be that humans are the first, or even the only "players" in the simulation, and the "gods" are the simulations' administrators needed to get humanity to a level where they could survive independently. Again, it doesn't matter which scenario is true; I think the ancient writings were attempts by people at the time to record how things started here. They are the **only** information that we have regarding "the beginning." If they are wrong, then we don't have any historical information at all, and we can just make up whatever fairy tales we like, which is what mainstream astrophysicists, archeologists, and evolutionists do.

CHAPTER 9

GOLDEN NUGGETS

Here's a very summarized list of little puzzle pieces I've accumulated over the years that led me to the conclusion of the simulation theory.

1. Physicists concluded quite a while ago that when you keep drilling down into the subatomic level of matter, you finally arrive at the point where "there's nothing solid there." As one physicist described it, at the lowest levels, reality seems to be like a movie screen—just interference patterns in an ocean of electromagnetic waves, exactly what you would expect from a simulation.

2. Psychologists recognized years ago that "it's all in your head." Read some information about how humans "see." There are some really fascinating experiments they've done with vision, and the results are mind-bending, such as having subjects wear glasses that change the colors they see, and with a little time the brain changes the colors back to what they should be. Or glasses that flip everything upside down and backwards and, again, with a little time the brain puts everything back to the way it should be. How does the brain "know" how things are supposed to appear? There are also fascinating studies on hearing. We "hear" notes in music that aren't actually there. Do a little research and look up those types of experiments/studies.

Light enters our eyes, hits the retina, and is converted to signals carried by the optical nerve to the brain. The image of what we "see" is actually a picture put together by the brain based on those signals, likewise with hearing, and touch, and taste, and smell. They are all just signals carried by nerves to the brain, which then interprets them into what we experience as reality. The key point is that the brain actually creates what we perceive as reality based on nerve impulses. Researchers realized long ago that if you could control the nerve signals going to the brain, you could create whatever "reality" you wanted, and the brain wouldn't know the difference.

3. In the middle 1980s, the government of Japan teamed up with many of the largest Japanese corporations and launched a ten-year project with the goal of creating a computer system that had the same capabilities as the human mind. For the first six years, they made good progress; in fact, they felt like they were ahead of schedule. But then they started running into difficulties and were, in the words of one of the project's top managers, "floundering around." After several months of floundering around, they stopped and analyzed the problem. From the analysis, they realized they had reached the limit of understanding how the brain worked. So, they changed their focus and spent the next several years figuring out how the brain works.

They theorized that, like a computer, the brain had a central command center. In their subsequent research that turned out to be true. They identified a central command center and several other processing centers that handled particular functions. Putting it in layman's terms, again in the words of that top manager, in the command center, they identified all the switches, knobs, and control mechanisms. But, as he said, it was what they couldn't find that ultimately ended the project.

From all their research, they concluded that the human brain is a "machine designed to be run by a ghost." Mind you, these are not religious people. This was their scientific conclusion. Once they realized that, and then spent some time confirming that conclusion, they finally ended the project because, in his words, they couldn't find, much less create, the ghost needed to run the machine.

I followed that project over the years and found the conclusion quite surprising. While I was always skeptical of their ability to accomplish the goal of creating a computer equal to the human mind, I wasn't expecting the project to wind up confirming the existence of a soul, "the ghost in the machine."

4. Another interesting line of research I read about was a medical researcher trying to find where memories are stored. While a college student studying to become a doctor, he read a paper by a researcher written years earlier that had concluded that memories weren't stored in the brain. The college student was a firm evolutionist believer that humans are nothing more than biological machines and he said the paper so

infuriated him that he made it his life's work to prove the author wrong. After fifteen years of research, he said that, to his great dismay, not only did he not prove the original author wrong, but he had proven beyond a shadow of a doubt that the original author was right. And not only were memories not stored in the brain, but he also proved they weren't stored anywhere else in the body either.

For me, this was another clue that things are not quite the way they appear. If memories are not stored anywhere in our bodies, then where are they stored? Our modern computer systems provide a great model for analogies. While writing this book on my computer, I can research all sorts of information on the internet. But if I looked through all the components of my computer, I wouldn't be able to find any of that information anywhere in my computer. How can that be? Of course, we all understand that that information is not actually stored in my computer. It's all stored somewhere out there on the internet, "in the cloud." Likewise, our memories are apparently stored in some "cloud"; i.e., somewhere else. Exactly where is that somewhere else?

5. Researchers in other disciplines have come to the conclusion that our brains are like transceiv-

ers. i.e., they transmit and receive information by some sort of signal that we currently can't detect. This is just like our phones that send and receive information from "the cloud." Apparently, like our computers and phones, our brains simply access our memories from wherever they are stored whenever we want or need them.

One microbiologist studied the pattern of little "bumps" on the outside of human cell walls. Apparently, these "bumps" are like fingerprints. They are unique to each person. For quite a while, researchers hadn't found any purpose for the bumps. But this microbiologist said he had finally figured out what they are. He determined that they're like antennas and are what allow the individual cell to communicate with the mind, soul, spirit, or whatever you want to call it that controls our brain and body. Each person has a unique "bump" pattern that correlates to their particular communication "signal," just like each cell phone has a unique ID that allows it to accept only the information signals that are meant for it.

6. Scientists have recognized for a while that the cells in our bodies are obviously being directed by an "intelligence" using some means of communication that they can't detect. For example,

when we get a cut, white blood cells will rush to the site of the cut to start repairing the damage. But they don't just randomly follow the normal flow of blood through the blood vessels until they just happen to go by the wound area. They take shortcuts and routes that get them to the wound in the least amount of time. They "know" there's a wound, and they "know" the shortest route to get there. Either the individual cells "know" or they are being guided by some sort of intelligence. Even the processes that happen inside an individual cell are not random; they, too, are done on purpose (intelligently).

Likewise, when an embryo is forming, the cells somehow "know" exactly how long to make a bone before they build the joint, and exactly how big to make a particular organ. Scientists have searched in vain for some sort of mechanism that could provide the "measurement" information that is needed for the individual cells to know exactly where to build what. Again, there is apparently some sort of intelligence directing the process that scientists haven't been able to find—just like the Japanese project team couldn't find the "ghost" that runs the brain.

7. One of the most interesting discoveries in physics is that the simple act of observing changes how electrons, photons, and other subatomic

elements behave. Physicists have found that on the "quantum level," things are in a type of "undefined state," which they describe as being like a "cloud of possibilities" until they are observed, which then causes them to "resolve" into a particular state.

One famous example is the "double slit experiment," in which light passes through a wall with two closely spaced slits. When it hits another wall on the other side, the light will create a brighter and darker interference pattern which looks like what waves of water would do passing through two openings. But it only does that as long as you can't tell which slit each photon went through. If you put a photon detector next to just one of the slits, then the interference pattern instantly disappears, and you wind up with just two bars of light on the back wall like we would naturally expect. This experiment and many others like it have been done thousands of times by lots of researchers. The net result is that, at the subatomic level, merely observing something affects, and even determines, the state of the elements. It's like the universe doesn't bother to "resolve" the subatomic activities unless they are being observed.

Current computer games utilize a similar tactic. They have large areas (maps) that the characters can move around in. But the game only processes the portion of the map that the player can see (observe) on the screen at any particular moment. In computer terms, it's called "rendering." Rendering requires a lot of computing power, and since there is no reason to render portions of the map that the player can't see, the computer doesn't bother, and consequently, it saves a lot of useless processing work. From what physicists have learned about the observer effect, it seems the universe is doing the same thing, only rendering the things that someone is observing.

8. In physics, there are a number of what they call "constants." Generally, constants are just a number or small equation that has to be plugged into a larger equation to make it "work"; i.e., match reality. For many of them, there isn't any physical explanation for why they exist. They're just there. I suspect that these constants are actually artifacts (the result of) of the underlying programming or processing system that creates the simulation we live in.

9. The physical sciences have no explanation for consciousness—where it comes from, how it could have developed, or even how it works. Yet it's all around us. It's kind of amusing to realize that insects with brains smaller than the head of

pin are conscious, but our most powerful super computers have not a shred of self-awareness. They have no emotions, don't care about anything, no sense of self preservation, no fear of being hurt or killed, and yet every animal on earth does.

So, what do all those little facts I just listed have in common? While I just listed them out in a very summarized form over the last couple of pages, I found those little gold nuggets (clues) over a period of quite a few years of reading and learning. I recognized when I read or heard each one of them that they were important pieces of the puzzle, and I tucked them away for future reference. As I accumulated them and pondered how they could fit together into some picture of reality, I finally realized they all point to the same thing: our universe is not quite as "real" as it appears to be. Try it for yourself. See if you can come up with an explanation that fits those little "golden nugget" facts.

If you ignore the characters and the plot, the best two examples I've seen of the simulation concept are the movies *The Matrix* and *Avatar*. In *The Matrix*, humans are trapped in a computer system that controls all of the signals going to their brains and creates a simulated world that the humans think is real. Their bodies are kept alive by using intravenous feeding and respirators, just like we keep people alive that are in a vegetative state today.

In *Avatar*, humans are in an alien world. They create cloned bodies of the alien world's natives and have technology that allows them to temporarily transfer their consciousness into one of the cloned bodies. (The clone bodies have no consciousness of their own.) In the cloned body, they can interact with the natives, hopefully, without the natives knowing they are actually beings from another planet.

(On a sidenote, in the movie *Avatar*, they can only take control of the cloned bodies they created. But if they could transfer their consciousness into, and take control of, one of the existing natives, you would have the exact same scenario referred to as "demon possession" in religious beliefs.)

I think the **concepts** these two movies are based on are in fact exactly how our universe works. The universe is a simulation just like the environment in role playing computer games, and our physical bodies are our avatars just like the characters in the computer games. The biggest difference between current games and "reality" is that **everything** we experience in our "reality" is from the perspective of the avatar in the game, whereas with our current computer games we are physically outside of the game and are still aware of our "real" environment. But using virtual reality technologies, our games are moving rapidly towards "total immersion," and I'm confident that it won't be too many more years before we'll have the technology to be completely "in the game" rather than just seeing it on a screen. In other words, while playing the game, everything we experience will be from the perspective of our game character—sight, sound, smell, touch, and taste. From there, it's just a matter of computing power and sophistication before our games will be indistinguishable from "reality." Stop and think about that for a moment. If we mere human mortals are capable of doing it, is it really that hard to believe that this is in fact a virtual reality?

It's quite interesting and amazing how well the simulation theory fits not only with current scientific knowledge but also explains many of the "mysteries" of religion. For example, where or what is "heaven"? Religions that believe in a heaven all agree that it's not an actual place in our universe. They view it as being outside of, and not part of, our physical universe. With simulation theory, that fits perfectly. Heaven is the "world" where our simulation was created. In religion, they call it the "spirit world." Likewise, the "Gods/angels/spirits" could just be people from that other world that aren't actually playing the game but are still interacting with our simulation.

UFOs and angels don't seem to be subject to the same laws of physics that we are. How can that be? It **could** be they are just a lot more technologically advanced than we are, or it could be that they are game "administrators" that are enabled to interact with the simulation but do not have to follow the normal rules of the game. In the movie *The Matrix*, the "agents" are a perfect example. Another example from modern computer games is called "cheats." Special programs are purposely designed to get around the limitations imposed by the game. Or they could also be like "abilities" characters in a game can acquire as they "level up" that give them capabilities and powers that the lower-level characters don't have.

Christians generally don't like the idea of our reality being a simulation, but it does explain a number of Biblical concepts, such as where the "angels" and "God" live and where the "soul" goes when we die. Multiple verses express the concept that some things on earth are just symbols or representations of things in "heaven." For example, various aspects of the tabernacle and temple are representative of things in "heaven."

Paul, referring to the future when he would be with God (wherever that may be), states, *"Now we see but a dim reflection as in a mirror; then we shall see face to face. Now I know in part; then I shall know fully"* (1 Corinthians 13:12). That could be understood as the difference in the perspective from within the simulation to the perspective from outside of the simulation. Interestingly, that's also right after the verse where he discusses talking, thinking, and reasoning like a child until he became a man and put away those childish things. From a child's perspective, our "reality" is the only true reality.

The Bible makes it quite clear that our "soul," although it "inhabits" (lives in) our physical bodies, is something separate from our bodies. In one verse, it describes our bodies as "clay vessels." This is exactly the same concept as in *Avatar*. Our consciousness (soul) "inhabits" the avatar but is something separate from the avatar. When the avatar "dies," our consciousness (soul) returns to "heaven" from where it came. Using the simulation theory, I believe that what most people think of as "heaven" is a fairly close definition of where we actually come from—and where we return to when we "die." Death is just the end of this game.

For Christians, our "world" could be understood as a simulation that "God" created to "test" the beings (humans) that he made, to see which ones He wants to allow into His "heaven" (i.e., where He actually lives) and those that He doesn't. By creating a simulation to test them in, there's no risk of the new beings messing up anything in His real world (heaven). In Mormonism, this world is believed to be a testing ground where the fallen angels are given a "second chance." They get to live as "humans" and have an opportunity to regain their place in "heaven." Again, the simulation concept fits perfectly with both of those scenarios. Humans would just be the avatars of the test subjects or the fallen angels.

On a sidenote, using the often-quoted statement in the Bible that "to God, a thousand years is like a day and a day is like a thousand years," I calculated the ratio of one day in "Gods" time equaling one thousand years in our "earthly" time. This could be seen as the difference in the passage of time between this "simulation" and the "real" time. It turns out that a human lifespan of about eighty years would equal about two hours of "real" time. I found that rather interesting. A lifetime on earth could be just two hours spent playing a game in the "real" world. Fascinating…

Assuming our universe is a simulation explains why researchers can't find where our memories are stored. Or the ghost that operates the brain. Memories are not stored there. They are stored in the "real" world, which is also where our consciousness (the ghost) comes from. It explains why, at the smallest level, physicists can't find any "real" matter. It's all just energy patterns, and they can't even figure out where the energy comes from. It's "just there."

The simulation explains how 90 percent of our body functions are totally automatic—temperature control, blood sugar levels, hormone levels, protein synthesis, and on and on. Not only do we not control them, we're not even consciously aware of them. It explains how animals have "instincts"—behaviors that they are apparently just "born with." If you raise a baby sparrow in your house to near adulthood and then take it outside, you will notice that it will immediately begin searching the sky for predators. Where did it learn that behavior? Why is it "naturally" afraid of other birds? How do bees automatically know how to build honeycombs? Why do they automatically go searching for pollen? These are just a tiny fraction of examples of "instinctual" behaviors we can observe in all sorts of creatures.

The answer is that automatic body functions and instincts are just pre-programmed functions built into the simulation. Life wouldn't be possible without them. How can "dead" molecules of the various elements from the elemental table combine into organic structures and a virtual stew of chemicals that all then "intelligently" and "automatically" work together perfectly to create the life forms we find all around us? How can they pass on instinctual knowledge from one generation to the next? This is like asking how electricity could "naturally" organize itself into high and low patterns that represent 0's and 1's and then "naturally" grow crystals into CPUs containing billions of logic gates that process those 0's and 1's into patterns that represent the words in this book. Of course, the answer is it can't. To believe it could would be completely irrational.

Likewise, to believe energy (that has no discernible source) just happened to organize itself into matter which then organized itself into stars, planets, and galaxies, which then just happened to spawn living cells, which then evolved into highly complex organisms, which then randomly developed self-consciousness is completely irrational. The lack of knowledge required to believe that would be astounding, which is why it's taught to children. Having no knowledge to be able to even question or evaluate what they are being taught, children just accept it as true. By the time they are old enough to be able to research and question such ideas, they have already believed them as facts for years. This is called indoctrination, and it is how 99 percent of people wind up with beliefs as adults that they have never questioned, researched, or examined. It's also how most people wind up with their religious beliefs.

CONCLUSION

Humans are born completely ignorant (which would be a necessary condition for us to believe that this world is "real"). It requires a certain level of knowledge before you can even realize you're ignorant. It requires a lot more knowledge to realize how many things you believe that have no factual foundation at all, that are, in fact, just stories someone told you.

Our conscious brains basically start as a blank slate—an empty vessel. Imagine for a moment a milk tanker trailer for a semi-truck. That big milk tank is like our brain. Initially, it's nice and clean and empty. As we go through life, information gets dumped into that big milk tank. Although the tank is made for milk, unfortunately a lot of the information that gets dumped in there is poop. Lies, misinformation, false stories, false beliefs we are taught, etc. Think for a moment about how willing you would be to drink milk that came from a tanker trailer that had poop in it. Yes, that's gross.

Yet that is exactly what we experience every day—mass information from television, radio, newspapers, social media, friends, family, teachers, and preachers. And a lot of that information is nothing more than poop. We grow up on a steady diet of poop-tainted milk. In fact, the vast majority of people are so used to poop-tainted milk that if they get a taste of pure, clean milk, they think there's something wrong with it. That's not what they're used to. It doesn't taste right. That's exactly what happens when most people hear the truth. It doesn't fit with all the crap they've been told. It doesn't sound right.

Are you content to keep drinking poop-tainted milk? If not, how do you clean out that milk tank? One thing you have to do is take all the contents of the milk tank and run it through a filter to remove all the poop. That means you have to examine your beliefs and assumptions and divide them into those that have a factual basis and those that don't. But that alone won't help much if you put the filtered milk back into a tank that still has poop built up on the walls and in the crevices.

So, while you are filtering the milk, you also have to find those poop deposits in the tank and clean them out. This is a process that takes time and effort. The more you learn, the more poop you will discover that needs to be cleaned out. So you need to keep filtering the information that is in your tank. At the same time, you must always be filtering new information that is being dumped into the tank. As your knowledge grows, your filters will get better, and your milk will become cleaner and purer. As you learn what clean pure milk tastes like, you will more quickly recognize poop when you read or hear it. It winds up being a self-reinforcing process. The better your filters, the cleaner the milk is. And the cleaner your milk is, the better your filters will become. The biggest hurdle is just getting someone to recognize that the "chocolate" milk they are used to drinking is not actually milk, but a bunch of crap mixed with milk.

The modern myth of Santa Claus has its foundation in a Greek man born in the late third century AD. He became the bishop of Myra, a small Roman town in modern-day Turkey. He was loved and admired by his community for his piety, kindness, and generosity and consequently became the subject of many legends (i.e., made-up stories). Some legends say he was a wealthy man that gave away all his money and traveled around helping the poor and sick. One story says he saved three poor sisters from being sold into slavery by providing their father with money to use as dowries so they could be married. Another story says he resurrected three boys that an inn keeper had murdered. Obviously it's a fantasy, but it shows how the stories get bigger and better. Over time, he became known as Saint Nicholas, the patron saint of children. December 6 is a festival day dedicated to him that is still celebrated in some European countries. December 25 is the day most of the world celebrates Christmas (Christ's Mass) and Santa Claus.

It's enlightening to consider all of the various aspects of the modern Santa Claus, such as his magical abilities, his home at the North Pole, his elvin helpers (angels?), flying reindeer, flying sleigh, and most importantly, his December 25 delivery of gifts to boys and girls all over the world. None of these things have anything to do with the original bishop of Myra, so where did all these stories come from? Well, they were all just made up over time as the myth of Santa Claus evolved into what it is today. Of course, no one argues that any of it is true. We all know it's just an excuse to have a holiday (Holy Day) in the middle of winter and a fun fantasy that we tell young children.

It's also interesting to note the similarities between Santa Claus and the Christian God. They're both loving and kind. They're both all-knowing. There's nowhere you can hide from them. They know if you're asleep or awake. They want you to be good and know whether you have or haven't been. They reward you if you've been good and deprive you or give you things you don't want if you haven't.

Like the myth of Santa Claus, modern Christianity is a made-up story very loosely based on a teacher and reformer named Yeshua. Today, there are a multitude of Christian rituals and holidays, virtually all of which have been adopted and modified from other "pagan" rituals and holidays. As most people know, Yeshua was not born on December 25, but we celebrate it as his birthday anyway. It turns out December 25 **was** the birthday of the "pagan" sun god Mithra. The religion of Mithraism was based on Sun worship. The first day of the week was named Sunday because it was the holy day of "Sun" worshipers. Easter comes from the worship of the Babylonian goddess Ishtar: the Great Mother, the Goddess of Fertility, and the Queen of Heaven. It was an ancient holiday held after the spring equinox to celebrate the return of spring. The Catholic church adopted it as the day of Yeshua's resurrection.

Just as the mythology of Santa Claus evolved, so did the beliefs and practices of Christianity. New made-up stories (philosophies, theories, dogmas) and practices were added over time. Yeshua would no more recognize the practices and beliefs of Christianity today than the original Saint Nicholas would recognize himself in our modern Santa Claus.

The truth is, just as our modern Santa Claus is just a bunch of made-up stories that were originally inspired by the bishop of Myra, the story of a long-prophesied messiah that was half God, half human, and was born on earth to redeem all sinners by being crucified and then was resurrected and ascended into heaven is just a made-up story inspired by the life and death of a reformer named Yeshua.

As I've pointed out throughout this book, there are no prophecies of a coming messiah in the Old Testament, there are many conflicting versions of the New Testament writings, the original New Testament writings have been provably altered and added to by unknown authors, and the authorship of many of the New Testament books can't be determined while it's provable from the writings themselves that the author ***is not*** the person officially credited. Finally, modern Christianity ***isn't even what Yeshua and his disciples actually taught***. They all practiced Judaism and taught their followers to obey the Old Testament laws, rules, and regulations (i.e., Judaism).

The idea that a single all-knowing, all-powerful, omnipresent being (God) was so lonely after creating millions of beings that praised, worshiped, sang to, and served Him continuously (the angels) that He created an entire universe, an earth, and then humans just so He would have someone to love and that would love Him back is more than a little hard to believe.

Then, when those new little beings learned the difference between good and evil, He was forced by His unfathomable righteousness to kick them out of the "garden" He had made for them, deprive them of the fruit of the Tree of Life, and condemn them to pain, suffering, and death. After a few thousand years, they had multiplied greatly and become so evil that He was sorry He had even made them in the first place (even though He supposedly knows the future) and had to drown the entire planet. But out of His great mercy, He saved eight of them so they could again multiply into millions more evil little creatures that needed slaughtering.

Then again, out of His great mercy, He "miraculously" impregnated one woman to bear His son, who was part God and part human who would then be unjustly killed so God could have a justifiable excuse to restore some of the humans to their original position and give them eternal life. In fact, we are told that this was the plan He had come up with before He even created the humans.

In the meantime, He creates a plan for every single human being's life. And for those that follow that plan, He tends to their needs, guides their path through life, counts the hairs on their heads, and comforts them when they're mistreated while He allows the Devil and evil people to rule so that everyone everywhere can see what the consequences of sin are.

Then He will send His crucified but resurrected son back to earth to slaughter two-thirds of all living humans and then rule over the rest for a thousand years. Finally, at the end of the thousand years, the millions of evil little beings will rebel one last time, and this time, God will destroy them all with fire, along with the earth itself. He will then judge each human that ever lived and divide them into two groups. The good ones get eternal life with Him, and the rest get thrown into hell. Then He will create a new, perfect earth with a heavenly city where everyone will live in peace and happiness for evermore. That's modern Christianity in a nutshell.

I truly wish there actually was a good, loving God that would reward good people and punish the evil ones. But that's not what we find. Whether we look at the present or throughout history, what we find is evil people ruling and destroying their fellow human beings. Every great once in a while, enough people will rebel that they successfully overthrow the evil ones, and for a time, things get better in their part of the world. But invariably, the scum rises to the top, and evil regains control. If there really was a good God ruling the earth, history would be far different.

Many people think that without the Bible or their favorite religious texts, there wouldn't be any basis or standard for determining right and wrong. But that, too, is false. **Everyone** knows what right and wrong is (if you believe the Bible, that's what we inherited from Adam and Eve). If you doubt everyone inherently knows right and wrong, then, without any justification, try killing a parent or sibling or child of a murderer. I can guarantee that the murderer would claim what you did was wrong. Steal from a thief, and the thief will angrily condemn what you did as wrong. Everyone knows right from wrong. That doesn't stop them from doing what they know is wrong, but they **do know** it's wrong—no God-given laws required. Furthermore, ignoring your conscience and doing things you know are wrong will have unpleasant consequences sooner or later. That's just cause and effect. Unfortunately, all too often the consequences come much later.

There are a lot of good morals, wise sayings, and educational examples in the Bible and other religious texts. There's also a lot of good historical information in them. Not all of it is 100 percent accurate, but there's often a kernel of truth if you can figure it out. So, while I've pointed out many things in the Bible that I believe prove it's not exactly the "Word of God," I do believe that it has educational value.

The point of this book is to, hopefully, keep people from following their religious beliefs to their logical conclusion. While it's true that you can believe pretty much whatever you wish, don't bet yours or anyone else's life on some kind, loving heavenly Father doing anything for you. Don't believe you will get forty virgins as a reward for killing yourself on a suicide mission to kill the infidels. In fact, don't risk anything you value on any God doing anything for you. Make your own decisions. Ethically, do what you can to achieve what you want. Pray all you want, but realize that it's no different than writing a Christmas wish list to Santa. Perhaps someone else may see your wish list and give something to you, but Santa isn't going to deliver.

After discussing the concept of this world being a simulation with a good Christian lady, I finally made this point. Put aside whether you actually believe it or not, and for just a moment, assume that what I'm saying is true. Then imagine that you died and, sure enough, you "awoke" and found out that it was all just a game that you'd been playing for a couple of hours. What would your immediate thought be? She laughed and said, "I would want to do it over and do it much differently." And I responded, "Exactly."

How would you live life if you knew it was just a game? Fear and worrying about what others think probably wouldn't hold you back. You wouldn't be looking for some invisible, magical being to help or guide you. You would learn how the game is played and then play it to the best of your ability. You would go for the gold medal. Dance like no one was watching. Enjoy the present, even the struggle. You wouldn't be devastated when you experienced difficulties or setbacks. Nor give up as long as you could still play effectively. You would be free of the things that hold most people back. The loss of a loved one wouldn't be such an agonizing soul-crushing experience if you understood that it was only their avatar that "died" and that they are back sitting on the couch in the "real" world, possibly watching to see how well you continue to play the game.

There was a millionaire businessman by the name of Jim Rohn. He was an excellent speaker who taught, recorded, and sold thousands of seminars and also wrote several books on how to live life successfully. In one of them, he tells of being hired by a big corporation to provide advice to the board. After talking to the board for a while, it became clear to him that what they wanted him to do was to tell them the political direction the country was heading over the next few years; in other words, tell the future.

Once he realized that, he used an analogy to explain to the board that they were asking the wrong question. He told them that running a business was like sailing a boat, and that what they were asking him was equivalent to asking which way the wind was going to blow. Then he said that there are two ways to sail a boat. One way is to kneel down on the bow and pray to whatever God you believe in to make the wind blow in the direction you want to go. He didn't recommend that method because very rarely was it successful. The other way is to actually learn how to sail the boat. As he explained, if you learn how to sail the boat, it doesn't matter which way the wind blows, you will still get to your destination.

I would encourage you to quit trying to get God to make the wind blow the direction you want to go. Live like this life is a game, not by being reckless, stupid or evil, but by realizing that it's just temporary and there's no point in living in fear, worry, or endless regret. Don't waste time asking, hoping, and believing that some magical God, Allah, or Santa Claus will work a miracle for you to make your life better. He won't. Do your homework. Research the history of those writings you believe in. Try doing some of the things those writings say will result in God doing something for you. See if it actually works. Then quit living in fear and trepidation. Be bold and courageous, and get up and do it for yourself. Learn how to sail your boat. Because that's the way this game works. Read, do the research, learn the truth, and the truth will set you free.

www.ingramcontent.com/pod-product-compliance
Lightning Source LLC
Chambersburg PA
CBHW070050080526
44586CB00013B/998